Managing Innovation and Operations in the 21st Century

by

Jose Arturo Garza-Reyes

Vikas Kumar

Juan Luis Martinez-Covarrubias

Ming K. Lim

CRC Press
Taylor & Francis Group
Boca Raton London New York

CRC Press is an imprint of the
Taylor & Francis Group, an **informa** business

A PRODUCTIVITY PRESS BOOK

CRC Press
Taylor & Francis Group
6000 Broken Sound Parkway NW, Suite 300
Boca Raton, FL 33487-2742

International Standard Book Number-13: 978-1-138-21472-9 (Hardback)

Library of Congress Cataloging-in-Publication Data

Names: Garza-Reyes, Jose Arturo, author.
Title: Managing innovation and operations in the 21st century / Jose Arturo Garza-Reyes, [and three others].
Description: Boca Raton, FL : CRC Press, 2018. | Includes index.
Identifiers: LCCN 2017010582 | ISBN 9781138214729 (hardback : alk. paper)
Subjects: LCSH: Industrial management. | Management science. | Organizational effectiveness. | Technological innovations--Management.
Classification: LCC HD31.2 .G37 2018 | DDC 658.5--dc23
LC record available at https://lccn.loc.gov/2017010582

Visit the Taylor & Francis Web site at
http://www.taylorandfrancis.com

and the CRC Press Web site at
http://www.crcpress.com

Printed and bound in Great Britain by
TJ International Ltd, Padstow, Cornwall

We dedicate this work to our families, whose love, constant

and unconditional support have served as source of

inspiration and strength to complete this book project.

Jose Arturo Garza-Reyes

Vikas Kumar

Juan Luis Martinez-Covarrubias

Ming K. Lim

Contents

SECTION II Understanding the External Context

SECTION III   Understanding the Internal Context

Preface

The globalized and current competitive business environment of the twenty-first century has brought ever more challenging pressures to the operations of organizations. In this century, operations are not only expected to contribute to the profitability and efficiency of organizations but also to serve as a platform to achieve contemporary organizational objectives that include customer satisfaction, quality, responsiveness, and sustainability. Therefore, neither operations managers nor organizations can be successful in achieving these objectives if they stick to the old assumptions and ways of designing, managing, and improving operations. In this scenario, innovation plays an essential role to ensure that operations contribute to the competitiveness of modern organizations and help them to overcome the challenges that the twenty-first century has brought to them. Thus, the purpose of this book is to allow business leaders, existing and potential operations managers, or all those interested in this subject, to acquire core skills in the field of operations and innovation management to understand and effectively promote competitiveness through the development or adoption of best practices in the design, management, and improvement of a company's operations as well as to deploy a culture based on innovation and continuous improvement.

We wrote this book based on our experience as industrialists, consultants, researchers, and academics, after working with all those organizations that wanted their operations and innovation activities to take a primordial role in their constant battle for competitiveness. Our experience made us realize that most operational issues and problems faced by organizations derive from the lack of core knowledge about operations and their poor interactions with other functions of the organization and the external environment that currently dominates the world's markets. For this reason, we have divided this book into three main sections: the first section provides an understanding of the general context of innovation and operations management (Chapters 1 and 2), the second section provides a review of the external environmental factors that play a role in the innovative management of operations (Chapters 3 and 4), and the third one focuses on the internal aspects that surround the management of operations in an innovative way (Chapters 5–10). By focusing on core and well-established principles such as the role of operations managers, design of products, processes and services, organizational culture and structure within the context of managing operations and contemporary topics such as the economics of innovation and operations management, innovative global supply chains, innovation and sustainability, among others, the readers of this book will:

- Gain knowledge of operations management concepts, business models, methods, tools, and best practices used by successful organizations to improve their operations.
- Understand how to apply operations management concepts in a real industrial context.
- Reflect upon and consider particular operational issues that have a direct impact on the competitiveness of contemporary organizations.

Some of the chapters have also been complemented with case studies that have been written by industrial and academic experts with vast experience in various areas of operations and innovation. These cases show the practical application of some of the concepts, methods, tools, and/or techniques reviewed in the chapter where they appear.

We hope this book serves as a good reference to all kinds of business leaders, existing and potential operations managers, or all those interested in this field.

Acknowledgments

We would like to thank our institutions for the support received to produce this work. Also, we would like to thank our publisher, Productivity Press, and its editorial team for assisting us with the publication of this book. Finally, we would like to express our deepest gratitude to our following colleagues who contributed to the enrichment of this work by sharing their knowledge and experiences in innovating in operations management through the additional case studies included in some chapters of this book:

- Balan Sundarakani, *Associate Professor and Programme Director at the University of Wollongong, UAE*
- Kristina Kim, *Marketing Specialist, Kyrgyzstan*
- Lefteris Andreadis, *Operations Project Manager at Meggitt Plc., UK*
- Mustafa Al-Balushi, *Six Sigma Master Black Belt at Oman Aluminum Rolling Company, Oman*
- Simon Peter Nadeem, *PhD Candidate at the University of Derby, UK*
- Tony Anosike, *Senior Lecturer at the University of Derby, UK*

About the Authors

Prof. Jose Arturo Garza-Reyes is a professor of Operations Management and Head of the Centre for Supply Chain Improvement at the College of Business, Law and Social Sciences, University of Derby, UK. He holds a PhD in Manufacturing Systems and Operations Management from the University of Manchester, Manchester, UK, an MBA from the University of Northampton, Northampton, UK, an MSc in Production and Quality from the Autonoma de Nuevo Leon University, Mexico, a postgraduate certificate in teaching and learning in higher education from the University of Derby, and a BSc in Mechanical Management Engineering from the Autonoma de Nuevo Leon University, Mexico. He has published a number of articles in leading international journals such as the *International Journal of Production Economics, International Journal of Production Research, Production Planning & Control, Journal of Cleaner Production, Supply Chain Management: An International Journal*, among others. He has also published over 60 articles in leading international conferences and two books in the areas of manufacturing performance measurement systems and quality management systems. He has participated as leading guest editor for special issues in *Production Planning & Control, Supply Chain Management: An International Journal, International Journal of Lean Six Sigma, International Journal of Lean Enterprise Research, International Journal of Engineering Management and Economics*, and *International Journal of Engineering and Technology Innovation*. He is currently serving in the editorial board of several leading international journals as well as has contributed as a member of the scientific and organizing committees in a number of international conferences. He is also cofounder and editor of the *International Journal of Supply Chain and Operations Resilience* (Inderscience). He has also led and managed international research projects funded by the British Academy, British Council and Mexico's National Council of Science and Technology (CONACYT). His research interests include general aspects of operations and manufacturing management, business excellence, operations and quality improvement, and performance measurement. He is a chartered engineer (CEng), a certified Six Sigma-Green Belt, and has over six years of industrial experience working as production manager, production engineer, and operations manager for several international and local companies in both the UK and Mexico. He is also a fellow member of the Higher Education Academy (FHEA) and a member of the Institution of Engineering Technology (MIET).

 **Dr. Vikas Kumar** is an associate professor in Enterprise Operations Management at Bristol Business School, University of the West of England (UWE), Bristol, UK. In the past he has worked for the Dublin City University Business School, Dublin, Ireland, Exeter Business School, Exeter, UK, and University of Hong Kong, Hong Kong. He holds a PhD degree in Management Studies from Exeter Business School, UK and a Bachelor of Technology (first class distinction) degree in Metallurgy and Materials Engineering from National Institute of Foundry and Forge Technology, Ranchi, India. He has published more than 150 articles in leading peer reviewed international journals and conferences including the *International Journal of Production Research, Expert System with Applications, Industrial Management & Data Systems, Computers & Industrial Engineering,* and *Production Planning & Control.* He serves on the editorial board of six international journals including *International Journal of Services, Economics and Management, International Journal of Manufacturing Systems,* and *International Journal of Lean Enterprise Research.* He is a cofounder and coeditor for the *International Journal of Supply Chain and Operational Resilience (IJSCOR).* He also serves as a scientific/technical committee member for a number of national and international conferences and is a reviewer of more than 10 international peer reviewed high rank journals. He has secured research funding of around £1 million from various research agencies including EPSRC, Innovate UK, British Academy, British Council and Newton Fund. He is an active member of the British Academy of Management (BAM) and European Operations Management Association (EurOMA). His current research interests include green and sustainable supply chain management, short food supply chains, process modeling, Lean and agile systems, and service operations management.

Dr. Juan Luis Martinez-Covarrubias is chief economist for the three regional assemblies in Ireland. He is involved in the formulation and monitoring of Regional Spatial and Economic Strategies within the Irish National Planning Framework. He is a research fellow at the University of Derby, Derby, UK. He holds a PhD in Industrial Economics and Policy Evaluation from the University of Limerick, Ireland, an MSc in Economic Competitiveness and International Business from the University of Birmingham, UK, a postgraduate diploma in Project Social Evaluation from the Technological Autonomous Institute of Mexico (ITAM), Mexico, and a BSc in Economics from the University of Guanajuato, Mexico. He has published a number of articles in leading international journals, such as *Regional Studies*. His research interests tend to address economics of innovation, technological change, global value chains, industrial economics, policy evaluation, and sustainability studies. He has presented numerous international conferences and keynote speeches. Prior to his academic career, he held senior roles in the national civil service in Mexico at the National Audit Office, Office of the President of Mexico, and the regional development ministry at the State of Guanajuato, Mexico, achieving important institutional changes such as improvement of national audit system and implementation of project social evaluation as a framework to support decision making and budget prioritization.

Prof. Ming K. Lim obtained his PhD in Manufacturing Systems from University of Exeter, UK, and BEng (Hons) in Manufacturing Engineering from University of Liverpool, UK. He is currently Professor of Supply Chain and Operations Management and Cluster Lead—Supply Chain Innovation and Sustainability at Coventry University, UK. His role is to lead a group of supply chain academics and researchers to create critical mass in supply chain research to raise the university profile in this field, and disseminate it to the international platform and the commercial sector. His research is multidisciplinary, integrating engineering, computer science, information technology, and operations management. Most of his recent research work revolved around Radio-frequency Identification (RFID) technology, incorporated with Industry 4.0, Internet of Things, cloud computing, and big data analysis. His other research expertise includes sustainable supply chain management, green/low carbon logistics, Lean and agile manufacturing, responsive and reconfigurable manufacturing/supply chain, meta-heuristics, cost and system optimization, system modeling and simulation. Prior to this role, he was Professor of Supply Chain and Logistics Operations and Head of Centre of excellence for Supply Chain Improvement at University of Derby, UK. He is the Founding Head of RFID Advanced Research Alliance (www.therfid.com). He has been working with companies from manufacturing and logistics sectors in enhancing production and supply chain competitiveness, as well as in the implementation of RFID technology. The industrial collaborative projects involve large organizations, such as Toyota, Rolls-Royce, DHL, National Health Service NHS, Unilever, Alliance Boots, Tesco Express, and Caterpillar, and a range of SMEs across different industries. He has secured various UK and EU research grants. He is currently co-editor-in-chief, *International Journal of Logistics Research and Applications* (Taylor & Francis), and editor-in-chief, *International Journal of Supply Chain and Operations Resilience* (Inderscience).

Section I

Understanding
the General Context

1

Understanding the General Context and Link between Innovation and Operations Management

1.1 INTRODUCTION

It is well accepted in the business world that every organization requires to constantly develop innovative business models, products, and services in order for them to remain competitive. However, as crucial as these innovations, innovative operations also need to be developed to produce and deliver such products and services on time, with the highest possible quality, and at the lowest possible cost. Nevertheless, innovation in operations is often overlooked. To meet this challenge, an understanding and integration of innovation activities within operation activities is essential. Here we focus on providing some general background on the management of operations and innovation activities, while at the same time emphasizing the role of the operations management function and operations managers in the current competitive environment.

The chapter also acknowledges the importance of innovation in the management of operations and urges organizations to integrate both activities as a vehicle to improve their operations. Therefore, we conclude this chapter by providing some general background on the different types of innovations and some insight into how the activity of innovation can be managed as a process.

1.2 UNDERSTANDING THE MEANING OF OPERATIONS AND INNOVATIONS MANAGEMENT

1.2.1 Importance of Operations Management

Operations management plays a significant role in all types and sizes of industries whether they are manufacturing or service organizations. In fact, the boundaries between manufacturing and services have been blurred with the growing offering of product service mix by most business organizations. This is largely driven by the intense competitive environment and tangible and intangible nature of the consumer demand. Revenues earned from services in many cases have overtaken manufacturing. As an example, the UK division of Rolls-Royce based in East-Midlands that specializes in aero engines generated 48% of its 2014 annual revenue from the sales of its engines, whereas 52% of the revenues were generated from the repair and maintenance aftersales services (Rolls-Royce Holdings Plc. 2014). This example shows the changing dynamics of the competition in the manufacturing sector. Operations management is sometimes also referred to as *production and operations management*, a term that was coined to blend and encourage the transfer of skills, techniques, and best practices between the manufacturing and service sectors. A number of examples from the industrial world show the growing dominance of service offering in the manufacturing sector that often provides the organizations a competitive edge (e.g., the aftersales repair and maintenance services provided to Rolls-Royce customers). The example of Rolls-Royce also shows that for many manufacturing organizations the core manufacturing activity is only one part of the operation involved in the production and delivery to its customers. Hence, organizations need to innovate and continuously improve their operational processes to sustain competitive advantage and meet their strategic objectives.

Over the years operations management has evolved as an important activity for improving the performance and profitability of any organization. Operations management helps organizations to achieve this by helping them to manage their resources and asset base efficiently, while simultaneously producing goods and offering services that satisfy their customers. A study by Slack et al. (2016) suggests that well-managed operations can provide four types of advantages to an organization:

- It can lead to the *reduction of the operational cost* incurred when producing products or delivering services.
- It can *improve customer satisfaction* by delivering good quality products and services, ultimately contributing to increasing revenues.
- It can lead to the *reduction of the capital employed (i.e., investment)* to produce or deliver the required type and quantity of products and services.
- It can *form the basis for future innovation.* This is expected as operations management focuses on continuously improving operations, resulting in the generation of new ideas, approaches, and technologies.

1.2.2 What Is Operations Management All about?

Operations management forms the central part of the successful functioning of any organization and often is referred to as the management of processes. Although this may give impression that operations management is just about management of processes within an organization, the boundaries of operations management span from the effective planning and control of the processes linked to conversion of an *input* to an *output*, as well as its design and improvement, that must be aligned to an organization's operations and corporate strategies. Therefore, the primary activities of operations management include the effective design, effective and efficient planning and control, and improvement of processes. Operations management relies on the fundamental concept of conversion/transformation of a set of input resources with the help of transforming resources into outputs of goods and services to satisfy specific customer needs. Some examples of these input–process–outputs for different types of organizations and industries are shown in Table 1.1. These examples show that every organization needs a conversion process to transform inputs into outputs to meet its customer needs. Following this notion, all organizations seem similar because they all use some form of inputs, which is transformed by a conversion process to produce an expected output, that is, product/services. This leads to the conclusion that operations form an integral part of every organization. Therefore, an easy way to gain a better understanding of your operations is to create a list of inputs, conversion processes, and outputs similar to the one shown in Table 1.1. The table shows that the organization can create a list at three different levels to obtain a micro or

TABLE 1.1

Examples of Operations Inputs, Conversion Processes, and Outputs

Organization	Input	Conversion Process Include	Outputs
TV Manufacturer	• Material (e.g., circuit boards, electronic components, plastic parts, glass, rubber, etc.) • People • Skills • Energy • Facilities	• Welding • Painting • Assembly • Testing/Inspection	• Televisions • Remote Controls
Warehouse	• Goods for storage • Equipment (e.g., information system, computers, fork trucks, etc.) • Staff • Storage facilities (e.g., racks, space, etc.) • Material	• Store goods • Management of stored goods • Transportation	• Goods kept on inventory
Hospital	• Doctors • Medicines • Knowledge • Patients	• Medical Operations • Consultations • Therapy	• Healthy patients
Logistics Company	• Fleet • People • Information System • Parts for repairs	• Uploading trucks • Transporting goods • Downloading trucks	• Goods moved from point "A" to point "B"
University	• Administrative staff • Academic staff • Classrooms • Computer labs • Teaching equipment	• Lectures • Tutorials • Seminars • Exams	• Knowledgeable Students

macro understanding of its operations, for example, to show the inputs, conversion process, and output of flow between resources (i.e., process level—a specific process within a department), flow between processes (i.e., peration level—specific process that moves across departments), and flow between operations (i.e., supply chain level—specific process across different facilities and/or organizations).

Any organization's assets base normally lies within the boundaries of the effective design, management, and improvement of such resources. Therefore, to remain competitive and succeed, it is vital for organizations to efficiently and effectively utilize their resources. Research has shown that innovation plays a major role in the design, management, and improvement of conversion processes (i.e., operations). Hence, organizations need to continuously innovate to outcompete their rivals and meet the expectation of their customers.

1.3 THE ROLE OF THE OPERATIONS FUNCTION AND OPERATIONS MANAGERS IN THE CURRENT COMPETITIVE ENVIRONMENT

1.3.1 The Operations Function

Most modern organizations assign work and group people based on different intra-organizational structures, and the most common way of doing this is through a structure based on function or purpose (e.g., production, marketing, human resources, finance, etc.). Since every organization produces some sort of product or provides services, they all have specific functions (i.e. departments) in charge for managing the resources that are dedicated to the production and delivery of the product or service. In basic terms, the role of the operations function is to produce the products for an organization's external customers and deliver services to them. As a result, the operations function is at the heart of any organization and hence it can be considered as one of the three core functions, along with marketing and new product/service development. However, the operations function is often referred to by different names in different organizations, which sometimes makes it difficult to identify. For example, in a manufacturing context the operations function is normally referred to as *production*, whereas in an organization maintaining and repairing aircraft, the operations function may be referred to as *aircraft maintenance, repair and overhaul (MRO) services*. In the distribution organization, the operations function may be referred to as *logistics* or *distribution*.

Regardless of the fact that the operations function is central to every organization, it needs support from other functions of the organization to operate effectively. Organizational support functions may include accounting, finance, marketing, human resources, among others. For instance, in a manufacturing environment, the production/operation function requires the support of other functions such as quality control, maintenance, production planning, warehousing management, and material handling to operate effectively. The important message to take from this discussion is that different organizations have different sets of support functions, and it is quite likely that these functions are referred to by different names. Additionally, the responsibilities and boundaries vary considerably from organization to organization, especially when compared interindustry and considering other characteristics such as size and where it is located. As a result, it is important to understand that operations and operational functions exist in all organizations although they may be present in different forms and shapes. Hence the identification of the processes and activities directly devoted to the production of the products and services provides a clear indication of the operations function within a specific company. This will be a normal way for you to identify the operations function within your own, or any other, organization.

1.3.2 The Operations Manager

Operations managers play an important role in managing operational functions within the organization; however, over the years their roles have changed considerably from simply implementing processes and driving efficiency gains to the point where they are now considered the primary engine driving an organization, and playing a critical role in formulation of its strategy. This changing role of operations managers is well acknowledged in the literature; for example, Paton et al. (2011) suggest that the role of operations managers is nowadays much more challenging, both in content and scope. They assert that the specific role depends on the type of the organization and characteristics of the industry where they work. Slack et al. (2016) and Paton et al. (2011) further suggest that besides the traditional tasks of designing processes and managing their capacity, in the current competitive environment, the other responsibilities of operations managers may include the following:

- Having an understanding of the organization's strategic objectives, contributing to the formulation of an organization's corporate strategy, and creating and implementing a supportive operations strategy.
- Formulating and implementing methods to improve organizational performance.
- Managing change to re-engineer, update, and improve the organization's processes to make sure that these meet the increasing market and competitive pressures.
- Designing products and services rather than simply been confined to their manufacture to an existing design, as it was done in the past.

In the present scenario, it is challenging for organizations to identify a set of skills that they need to develop in their operations managers in order for them to be effective, given that the scope of operations has widened, creating mergers and overlaps with other areas and functions of an organization. Therefore, operations managers are expected to have skills that would allow them to interact across various organizational areas and functions as suggested by Paton et al. (2011). This notion is very relevant for engineering- and manufacturing-oriented industrial sectors such as aerospace, automotive, and railways, where operations managers need to be able to effectively manage processes, people, and complexity. Organizations therefore must make sure that individuals pose some explicit *basic* traits; otherwise, they will not be able to develop a high impact career in operations management, and the organizations will not gain maximum benefit from their employees. Paton et al. (2011) refer these *basic* traits as follows:

- Ability to coordinate large numbers of tasks
- Ability to process large amount of varied and complex information
- Ability to solve complex and diverse problems
- Ability to effectively prioritize both timescale and criticality
- Ability to work under pressure while performing all the previous tasks and still meeting quality, time, and cost targets

Similar to the operations function, in some organizations an operations manager can be known as *administrative manager* (e.g., in a hospital), *fleet manager* (e.g., in a distribution or logistics company), *store manager* (e.g., in a supermarket), *production manager* (e.g., in a manufacturing company), and so on.

1.4 RECOGNIZING THE IMPORTANCE OF INNOVATION IN THE MANAGEMENT OF OPERATIONS

As discussed earlier, operations management is not only about planning and controlling processes to meet customer needs through the production or delivery of products and/or services, but it also involves designing and improving such processes. Therefore, every operations manager aims at constantly improving the existing processes of his/her organizations. It is at this point where innovation and operations management intersect. Innovation is often linked to the design of new products or services. However, innovation can play a key role in designing and improving existing operations and practices, for example, to improve efficiency, reduce waste, seek new customers, and increase profit. It is important to clarify here that the improvement of operations can generally be achieved in two different ways, through continuous improvement (i.e., kaizen) or through operational innovation (i.e., breakthrough). Continuous improvement refers to seeking incremental improvements on existing operations: ensuring that work is done as it ought to be to reduce delays, costs, and errors but without fundamentally changing how the operation is performed, whereas operational innovation refers to coming up with entirely new ways to achieve the same improvements, but in a shorter term and more dramatic way. More discussions on these two approaches to improvement and their suitability to specific situations will be presented in the subsequent chapters.

An important question that emerges is: what are the benefits for organizations to be innovative in their operations? Hammer's (2004) work provides evidence to this question in which he studied three cases: Wal-Mart, Toyota, and Dell, and reported that for these organizations operational innovation has been fundamental to their success. Wal-Mart is a classic example of operational innovation. They pioneered various innovations to improve their purchasing and distribution operations, and amongst them the best known operational innovation they developed is *cross-docking*. In this innovative distribution mode, goods transported to a distribution center from suppliers are directly transferred to trucks bound for stores, thus reducing the need to be stored in a warehouse. As a result of cross-docking, Wal-Mart managed to lower inventory levels and operating cost, which helped them to offer lower prices to their customers and outcompete their rivals. However, Hammer (2004) suggests that other factors such as effective strategy, culture, and human resources policies also played a critical role in the success of Wal-Mart, though much of it is attributed to cross-docking, and other, operational innovations. Similar examples can be found in Toyota and Dell, whose operational innovations such as the Toyota's Production Systems (TPS) and Dell Business Model have revolutionized how to run operations not only in their respective industries but beyond as well. For example, the TPS, which was initially designed and developed for manufacturing industries, has now been adopted in other industries such as construction, communications, health care, and education. These success stories are well documented in the literature, and in some cases they have even contributed to the complete change of managerial paradigms (e.g., in the case of the TPS from mass production to Lean manufacturing) and have also demonstrated the importance and need for organizations to seek both continuous and operational innovation improvements in their operations. This provides a good reason why your own organization must develop a culture that always pursues and seeks operational innovations. One should realize that operations managers are instrumental in contributing to the development of such culture that promotes innovation and identifying and implementing such improvements.

1.5 TYPES OF INNOVATION

Two well-known classifications of innovations in industry include both major (i.e., radical) and minor (i.e., incremental) innovations. The examples discussed in the previous section on Wal-Mart, Toyota, and Dell provide a good example of the radical and incremental innovation in the development and implementation of their operational innovations involved that has resulted in considerably wider organizational changes to accommodate such innovations. The substantial changes occurred not only in the operations function (i.e., production/manufacturing for Toyota and Dell and distribution and logistics for Wal-Mart), but also in other support functions such as material handling, production planning, and distribution control, maintenance, warehousing management, quality control, and so on. For instance, Toyota had to re-educate its suppliers to accommodate the delivery of smaller volume but more frequent deliveries to comply with one of the key elements of the TPS, that is, the just-in-time (JIT) approach. In addition, Toyota had to re-align its internal systems to control and handle raw materials, space storage, production equipment, and so on to match with the new TPS approach.

Together with the introduction of managerial approaches such as autonomation, 5S, and total productive maintenance, a totally new culture based on waste reduction had to be implemented by the company's staff that can serve a basis for this operational innovation. Therefore, thriving culture supportive of operational innovation also requires additional managerial and organizational changes. Consequently, it is imperative for companies to identify the importance of operations improvement through any innovative means that can require the need to accommodate new technologies, managerial practices, policies working methods, and so on that assist operational changes. Table 1.2 presents different types of innovations derived from operational innovation.

There are other types of innovation such as product innovation that may not necessarily be derived from operational innovations but from the need to improve other functions including product innovations (e.g., the development of a new or improved product) and commercial/marketing innovations (e.g., new financing arrangements, new selling approaches

TABLE 1.2

Types of Innovations Derived from Operational Innovation

Type of Innovation	Example
Organizational innovation	An introduction of a new working procedure or policy, a new communication system
Managerial innovation	Lean manufacturing, Total quality management (TQM), Six Sigma, Total Productive Maintenance (TPM), Autonomation
Operational innovation	Toyota production system, quality circles, JIT, new inspection procedure, takt time, pull system, Kanban
Process innovation	The development of a new manufacturing process or approach. For example, JIT was introduced in all Toyota's processes to aim at receiving parts and inventory at the right time when it was needed (i.e., not before or after)
Service innovation	Internet-based financial services, new service schedule based on Lean thinking (e.g., smaller but more frequent servicing)

such as direct marketing, etc.). However, in case of product innovation, it is important to indicate that when this innovation happens, it is mostly followed by operational innovation. Furthermore, the improvement in the operations is mainly performed by adjusting the manufacture of new products as opposed to improving the operation itself.

In summary, this section suggests that organizations must be ready to support the changes in their functional areas resulting from the implementation of operations improvements and innovations.

1.6 MANAGING INNOVATION AS A PROCESS

Managing innovation is a challenging task as innovation often includes a series of interlinked activities or processes. Organizations can always develop novel ways to resolve their operational problems; however, if the interlinked processes are not well realized, often the results of these efforts can become zero. Therefore, considering innovation as an isolated and independent event is a mistake. A study by Hammer (2005) reports that many organizations perform separate innovation activities in isolation such as brainstorming sessions, piloting projects, and campaigning and communicating with the market, hoping that these activities will complement each other at the end, but rarely this happens. Therefore organizations need to see innovations as processes or, in other words, a series of sequential steps and activities required to generate improvement ideas, and convert such ideas into actions that are put into practice in an organization's operations.

Paton et al. (2011) suggest that the process of innovation involves selection of high potential ideas that form the pool of ideas that are first generated, gathered, channeled, and absorbed. Therefore, organizations involved in operational innovation must first focus on generating innovative ideas to solve specific operational issues or improve an existing operation. This is normally considered as the first stage of the innovation process that in most cases is random and disordered. As a result, organizations should first focus on achieving order from this randomness, and this can be achieved by the effort to dedicate resources in developing ideas of high potential. Paton et al. (2011) suggest that each idea must be evaluated based on its implementation practicality, that is, *can it be done?* or *can it be implemented?* and for its effectiveness to improve an operation such as *will it help to overcome the problem tackled or achieve the desired improvement*? We do not intend to explore this step in detail as there are plenty of materials focused on different types of organizations and evidence of those can be found in the abundant list of research studies, see for example, Rainer (2014), Ness (2012), Lager (2010), and Shavinina (2003). The next step of the innovation process is the selection of high potential ideas.

The selected high potential ideas are then subjected to a design stage where these are further developed from a conceptual state to a practical state. At this stage, operations managers would finalize the conceptual idea into an applicable tool (e.g., device, managerial method, etc.) to support the improvement of the operation. For instance, an operations manager may come up with an innovative idea centered on a *poka-yoke* (error proof) device to reduce the amount of defects in one of the operations. The use of a specific poka-yoke device to tackle the problem is in itself the initial idea as to how to solve the problem (stage 1). Therefore, the next stage in the innovation process would be to design the poka-yoke device, implement it, analyze the outcomes, and make any necessary adjustments. If this is successful and no problems are encountered, the idea (i.e., in this case the poka-yoke device) can be fully implemented. As highlighted earlier, this operational innovation can result in other innovations, for example, a new managerial procedure may need to be devised and implemented to accommodate the introduction of a new piece of equipment in the operations. It is the task of the operations manager to ensure that all the different elements required to implement the operational innovation are in place so that expected benefits can be achieved.

Most innovation processes follow these two stages of idea generation and implementation; however, contingent to the magnitude of the improvement sought, ideas generated, and their potential application, the complexity and duration of the stages may vary. For example, operational innovations to solve prolonged problems well embedded within a company's operations and culture may take much longer than the relatively simple quality problem tackled with the poka-yoke device.

In a nutshell, the above-mentioned arguments suggest that operations managers need to continuously create and facilitate process-based operational innovation activities, instead of singular and isolated activities, to enhance the opportunities to succeed.

1.7 SUMMARY

Although we fully agree and undoubtedly recognize that organizations require to constantly improve and develop innovative business models, products, and services to remain competitive, in this chapter we have tried to encourage them to not only aim at effectively and efficiently managing their operations but also improving them through innovation and continuous improvement. This will allow them to successfully overcome some critical and contemporary challenges such as producing and delivering products and services on time, with the highest possible quality, and at the lowest possible cost. Considering the need for this, in this chapter we aimed at providing some general background and understanding in relation to the management of operations and innovation activities, while at the same time emphasizing the role of the operations management function and operations managers in the current competitive environment. The chapter has also acknowledged the importance of innovation in the management of operations. We concluded by providing some general background on the different types of innovations and some insight into how the activity of innovation can be managed as a process.

After having understood the general context and link between innovation and operations management, the following chapter will look at the economics of these activities.

KEY POINTS TO REMEMBER

- In the simplest possible form, an operation can be described as a transformational activity/process comprising inputs and outputs performed by transforming resources on transformed resources.
- Operations management contributes to the success of an organization by helping it to manage the operations resources and assets base effectively and efficiently, while still producing goods and services in a way that satisfy its customers.
- The main activities involved in the contemporary management of operations include the effective design, planning and control (i.e., management), and improvement of processes.

- Innovation and continuous improvement within the operations function are vital for any organization of any kind, and sector, to be competitive and achieve its strategic objectives.
- Therefore, it is essential for organizations to understand and integrate both innovation and operation activities.
- Operations and innovation activities intersect when attempting to improve the first (e.g., improving efficiency, cutting down waste, finding new customers, increasing profit, etc.).
- The improvement of operations can generally be achieved in two different ways, through continuous improvement (i.e., kaizen or incremental) or through operational innovation (i.e., breakthrough or radical).
- To be more effective, innovation should be managed as a process, or in other words, as a series of sequential steps and activities that need to happen to generate an improvement idea, and turn such an idea into actions that are put into practice in an organization's operations.
- Activities of the innovation process include: (1) generation of innovative ideas that may solve a specific operational problem or seek the improvement of an operation, (2) idea evaluation, (3) idea selection, (4) design stage to move the idea from a conceptual to a practical state, (5) implementation of the design, (6) analysis of the results, (7) making adjustments if necessary.
- The innovation process, in most of the cases, goes through these stages, but depending on the magnitude of the improvement sought, ideas generated, and their potential application, the complexity and duration of the stages may vary.

REFERENCES

Hammer, M. (2004). Deep change: How operational innovation can transform your company. *Harvard Business Review* 82(4): 84–93.

Hammer, M. (2005), Making operational innovation work. *Harvard Management Update* 10(4): 1–7.

Lager, T. (2010). *Managing Process Innovation: From Idea Generation to Implementation*. London, UK: Imperial College Press.

Ness, R. (2012). *Innovation Generation: How to Produce Creative and Useful Scientific Ideas*. New York, NY: Oxford University Press.

Rainer, G. (2014). *Think Fast Act Faster: How to Generate Innovative Ideas and Make Them Happened*. Singapore: Rank Books.

Rolls-Royce Holdings Plc. (2014). Annual report 2014—better power for a changing world. Available at: http://www.rolls-royce.com/investors/financial-results/annual-report.aspx#yr-2014-annual-report (10 August 2015).

Paton, S., Clegg, B., Hsuan, J., Pilkington, A. (2011). *Operations Management*. Berkshire, UK: McGraw-Hill.

Shavinina, L. (2003). *The International Handbook on Innovation*. Oxford, UK: Elsevier Science.

Slack, N., Brandon-Jones, A., Johnston, R. (2016). *Operations Management*, 8th Edition. Harlow, UK: Pearson.

FURTHER SUGGESTED READINGS

Hammer, M. (2004). Deep change: How operational innovation can transform your company. *Harvard Business Review* 82(4): 84–93.

Hammer, M. (2005). Making operational innovation work. *Harvard Management Update* 10(4): 1–7.

Hill, A., Hill, T. (2012). *Operations Management*, 3rd Edition. London, UK: Palgrave Macmillan.

Paton, S., Clegg, B., Hsuan, J., Pilkington, A. (2011). *Operations Management*. Berkshire, UK: McGraw-Hill.

Tidd, J., Bessant, J. (2013). *Managing Innovation: Integrating Technological, Market and Organizational Change*, 5th Edition. West Sussex, UK: John Wiley & Sons.

Trott, P. (2017). *Innovation Management and New Product Development*, 6th Edition. Harlow, UK: Pearson Education Ltd.

2

Economics of Innovation
and Operations

2.1 INTRODUCTION

Innovation has been widely recognized as one of the most important drivers to achieve competitiveness and growth at any level of analysis— either for the firm, for the industry, or for the nations. This chapter can be helpful for operations managers and anybody who wants to improve the operations and processes of their organizations through innovations. By bringing an economic perspective to this book, this chapter offers a brief review of the most important theoretical underpinnings that helps to understand what innovation is, its aspects, and implications. Section 2.2 presents an account of the theoretical foundations and aspects of innovation stressing the economics viewpoint and the evolutionary theory. A definition of innovation is provided that serves to understand this complex process. By doing so, certain types of innovation are identified. Section 2.3 explores the effects of innovation with emphasis on technological change. This section provides an account of historical clusters of innovation offering foundations to highlight the significance of innovation to the wider economic progress achieved worldwide. This chapter adopts a general and theoretical approach. It offers foundations helpful to engage in further chapters. The remaining chapters adopt a more practical approach by exploring how innovation is related to more specific issues, such as location, global supply chain management, culture, organizational structure, new product/service and processes design, and sustainability. Case studies offer means to better grasp these important issues.

2.2 THEORETICAL FOUNDATIONS (ASPECTS) OF INNOVATION

This section delves into the theories of the firm with a strong emphasis on innovation. This will allow operations managers who intend to improve the operations of their companies through innovation to acquire an overall knowledge on this complex process that—if designed and implemented adequately—will give him/her an edge and a source of competitive advantage to his/her organization. It presents a framework for understanding the evolution in economic thought from the neoclassical point of view to innovation economics.

Innovation is a complex concept that needs a multiperspective approach. Innovation is extremely important in the real economy and operations of organizations, and its study entails more than microeconomic principles. Understanding innovation requires some appreciation of evolutionary economic theory.

2.2.1 Economic Theories to Explain Innovation

Economics of innovation is a central part to understand innovation and technological change, and its effect on firms, industries, competition, and our societies. The study of economics can be guided by different schools of thought, including neoclassical, Keynesian, and more recently, economics of innovation. Economics of innovation puts innovation at the center of the economic activity analysis. Schumpeter (1928, 1934, 1947) is considered a pioneer of this discipline, followed by other contributors, such as Romer (1990), Nelson and Winter (1974), Metcalfe (1995), and Audretsch and Thurik (2001). Schumpeter (1943, p. 83) coined the term *creative destruction*, arguing that

> The fundamental impulse that sets and keeps the capitalist engine in motion comes from the new consumers' goods, the new methods of production or transportation, the new markets... [This process] incessantly revolutionizes the economic structure within, incessantly destroying the old one, incessantly creating a new one. This process of Creative Destruction is the essential fact about capitalism (Schumpeter 1943, p. 83).

The economics of innovation sees innovation as the key engine for growth (Kuznets 1973), as opposed to neoclassical economics, which assumes that the source of economic growth is the efficient allocation of scarce resources.

A starting point to understand innovation is through the theory of the firm (Demsetz 1991). Several streams in the literature attempt to explain the origins of the firm, as well as its nature, causes, and effects (Chandler 1992b). This section addresses the underpinnings of each theory, starting with neoclassical, touching on managerial, principal-agent, behavioral, stakeholder, co-operative game, transaction cost, and finishing with evolutionary theory. This will provide operations managers with an understanding of the nature of the firm and to highlight the importance of innovation for its success.

The neoclassical theory considers the firm as a *black-box* automaton, which pursues profit maximization. It transforms atomized inputs into marketable outputs, operating in a spaceless and timeless environment (Walras 1874, Jevons 1879, Marshall 1890). This perspective has strong explanatory power in the case of pure and perfect competition. This is also linked to operations management, which is understood as activities that help companies to produce the products and/or services that will be sold to customers. However, the profit maximization argument of the neoclassical theory loses validity in the absence of perfect information, and due to the complexity of organizations (Andreosso and Jacobson 2005).

O'Sullivan (2000) outlined deep criticism about the neoclassical theory and its failure to explain innovation. The author compared three main features of innovation to three characteristics of the resource-allocation process according to neoclassical theory. On the one hand, the innovation process is: (1) cumulative, moving toward the accumulation of the stock of knowledge; (2) collective—several participants learn and benefit from the innovation; and (3) surrounded by uncertainty, because future possible states of the world are unknown. On the other hand, the resource-allocation process is: (1) reversible, meaning that the equilibrium achieved by resource allocation today has no effect on tomorrow's allocation; (2) based on individuality—participants do not coordinate with each other, and each one acts in his or her own best interest according to the utility maximization function; and (3) optimal, implying choice among known alternatives. This comparison of features makes it easy to see why innovation does not fit into the neoclassical economics framework (Lazonick 2010).

Given the drawbacks of the neoclassical paradigm (imperfect information, complexity of organizations, and exogenous technological change), alternative theories of the firm emerged. These include managerial (Baumol 1967, Berle and Means 1932, Douma and Schreuder 1992), principal-agent (Fama and Jensen 1983, Williamson 1985), behavioral (March and Simon 1958,

Simon 1960), stakeholder (Freeman 1984), co-operative game (Aoki 1984), and transaction cost (Coase 1937, Williamson 1985).

All these alternatives to the neoclassical perspective fall short of explaining the relevance of technological change (Auerbach 1989, Lazonick 1991). Technological change gained considerable attention during the 1990s and early 2000s, when terms such as *the new economy*, *the knowledge economy*, and *the information society* were coined. This focus caused a shift in theoretical economic thinking toward endogenous growth models. These models considered technological change as a variable with a strong explanatory power for economic performance; therefore, they integrated a proxy for technological change/innovation into the production function (Korres 2016).

The endogenous growth models emerged in two main streams as alternatives to neoclassical theory. The first, evolutionary or neo-Schumpeterian economics (Schumpeter 1928, 1934, 1939, 1943, 1947), departs radically from the neoclassical tradition. The second, a range of neoclassical-based endogenous growth models, dispenses with some neoclassical elements (such as pure and perfect competition) while keeping other elements (such as marginal behavior). These neoclassical endogenous growth models are more applicable to macroeconomic analysis, displaying a limited explanatory power to address a microeconomic perspective (Wahid 2002). Evolutionary theory, presented below, is analyzed in more detail given its greater power to explain the innovation phenomena and why firms engage in innovation.

2.2.1.1 Evolutionary Theory

Evolutionary theory radically departs from the neoclassical perspective. Chandler (1990, p. 593) argues that "…economists, particularly those of the more traditional mainstream school, have not developed a theory of the evolution of the firm as a dynamic organization." In contrast, the evolutionary perspective adopts contributions from other theories, such as transaction cost theory. It considers the contribution of Williamson with regard to the firm-specific assets and skills of the firm, but differs as to the basic unit of analysis (Chandler 1992a); whilst the unit of analysis for Williamson is the transaction, from the evolutionary perspective it is the firm itself and its asset specificity (physical and human assets). According to the evolutionary theory, the main features of the firm are strategy, structure, and core organizational capabilities. Organizational capabilities are defined as the spare managerial capacity of a firm, such as knowledge, experience, and skills, within the firm. Additionally, the evolutionary theory considers organizational routines, which are vital for competition and survival of the firm. Clark and Juma (1987, p. 59) suggest that "...routine is the genetic code of the firm, which carries the adaptive information necessary to compete and survive." Supporting this assertion, Nelson and Winter (1982, p. 99) affirm that routines are the firm's organizational memory. Routines and capabilities are not the same—organizational routines are a subset of the firm's capabilities. Although these routines influence the firm, they do not fully determine what the firm is capable of achieving (Dosi et al. 2001). Routines refer to what a firm actually does, whilst capabilities refer to what the firm is capable of doing if its resources are reallocated (Robertson and Langlois 1994). The evolutionary theory provides an explanation for the success of certain firms; it emphasizes that continuous learning makes the assets of a firm more dynamic, allowing the firm to gain sustainable competitive advantages.

Finally, according to evolutionary theory, individual or team competences (such as skills and tacit knowledge which are fostered and maintained within the organization) explain the existence, structure, and boundaries of the firm (Hodgson 2002). In contrast to transaction cost theory and principal-agent theory, which base their analyses of the firm on contracts and transactions, here the firm is explained by internal competencies that inform discussions of its conduct and behavior.

The evolutionary theory provides a consistent and robust theoretical framework for understanding the innovation phenomenon, which is one of the core concepts of this book. We turn now to address what actually innovation means.

2.2.1.2 Definitions of Innovation

Schumpeter succinctly defined innovation as "...simply the doing of new things or the doing of things that are already being done in a new way" (Schumpeter 1947, p. 151). The implication of Schumpeter's general definition is that innovation is not necessarily scientifically driven. Later, Dosi (1988) further developed Schumpeter's concept focusing on products, process, and organizational issues. He redefined innovation as

> ...the search for, and the discovery, experimentation, development, imitation and adoption of new products, new production processes and new organisational set-ups (p. 222).

Fagerberg et al. (2005) contribute with a clarification of the concept by contrasting *invention* against *innovation*. For Fagerberg et al., "invention is the first occurrence of an idea for a new product or process, while innovation is the first attempt to carry it out into practice" (p. 4). This definition clearly specifies the practical nature of innovation; hence the importance of firms as a natural environment for innovation to emerge.

A more commonly accepted definition of innovation is offered by the Organization for Economic Cooperation and Development (OECD 2005). The strength of this definition is that it enables the concept to be translated into practice

> The implementation of a new or significantly improved product (good or service), or process, a new marketing method, or a new organisational method in business practices, workplace organisation or external relations (p. 46).

This definition leads to a distinction between four types of innovation: product, process, marketing, and organizational. These are some types of basic and general definitions adopted by the Organisation for Economic Co-operation and Development (OECD 2005) and its member states for international comparison purposes. However, Chapter 1 provides a more specific typology focused on operations innovation. For the time being, the reader can bear in mind these general definitions.

> A *product* innovation is "…the introduction of a good or service that is new or significantly improved with respect to its characteristics or intended uses. This includes significant improvements in technical specifications, components and materials, incorporated software, user friendliness or other functional characteristics" (p. 48).

There are other subtypes of product innovation such as *pure product innovation*, *service innovation*, and *innovative pricing* (price discrimination) to name a few.

> A *process* innovation is "…the implementation of a new or significantly improved production or delivery method. This includes significant changes in techniques, equipment and/or software" (p. 49).

Subtypes of process innovation refer to *flexible manufacturing* and *product variety*.

A *marketing* innovation is "…the implementation of a new marketing method involving significant changes in product design or packaging, product placement, product promotion or pricing" (p. 49).

Finally, an *organizational* innovation is "…the implementation of a new organisational method in the firm's business practices, workplace organisation or external relations" (p. 51).

All these definitions have been widely accepted at an international level among policy makers and organizations, as they have been useful to implement innovation policies aimed at improving the performance of their economies. However, other typologies emerge depending upon the application and context. For instance, given the realm of operation management focused at a microeconomic level, on how firms operate and perform, then it is interesting to see the emergence of other types of innovation such as operational innovations. As mentioned earlier, a typology of innovations from operations management perspective is presented with more detail in Chapter 1.

Some features of innovation emerge. For instance, in terms of scope, innovations can be incremental—with minor, but consistent changes over the time—or radical, disruptive innovation that significantly changes functions, perceptions, and paradigms. In succeeding chapters, we discuss in more detail the effects of these characteristics of incremental and radical innovation on the operations of organizations. Innovation requires information and knowledge to emerge.

2.2.2 Knowledge as Driver for Innovation

Knowledge pays a significant role in innovation activity; therefore, it is important to review the perspective of knowledge-based view (KBV) of the firm. Originating from the strategic management literature, this perspective builds upon and extends the resource-based view of the firm (RBV) initially promoted by Penrose (1959) and later expanded by other contributors (Barney 1991a, 1991b, Wernerfelt 1984).

Grant (2006, p. 207) acknowledged that KBV is "…not a theory of the firm in any formal sense, …it is more a set of ideas about the existence and role of the firm that emphasize the role of knowledge." This set of ideas is built upon assumptions and observations concerning the nature of knowledge and its role in production. First, assumption with regard to the overwhelmingly high importance of knowledge as production resource in terms of market value and the primary resource of Ricardian rents (Grant 1996, Machlup 1980). Second, the different types of knowledge, that is explicit and tacit knowledge, have different effects on its transferability (Kogut and Zander 1992, Nonaka 1994). Explicit knowledge can be articulated and easily communicated between individuals and organizations. In contrast, tacit knowledge is transferred costly and slowly from one individual to another, and this knowledge is manifest only in its application. Third, knowledge is subject to economies of scale and scope, as its initial creation is costlier than its subsequent replication. The extent of these economies of scale and scope vary considerably between different types of knowledge. Large economies of scale and scope may be achieved with explicit knowledge, where information is "costly to produce, but cheap to reproduce" (Shapiro and Varian 1999, p. 3). In a different degree, tacit knowledge tends to be costly to replicate, but these costs are lower than those incurred in its original creation (Winter 1995). Fourth, there is need of specialization when creating and storing knowledge due to human nature. Efficiency in knowledge production requires that individuals specialize in particular areas of knowledge (Grant 1996, Simon 1991). Fifth, typically the production of a good or service requires the application of many types of knowledge (Kogut and Zander 1992).

Knowledge thus emerges as a key element enabling successful innovations. The seminal contribution of Cohen and Levinthal (1990) is helpful to see the relationship between knowledge and innovation. They coined the term *absorptive capacities* and defined it as: "...prior related knowledge which confers an ability to recognize the value of new information, assimilate it, and apply it to commercial ends" (p. 128), which basically is innovation.

2.2.2.1 KBV and Evolutionary Economics

KBV is compatible with evolutionary economics. In line with Nelson and Rosenberg's (1993) definition of innovation (i.e., as the process by which firms master and put into practice new product designs and manufacturing processes), it has to be understood as a process in which new knowledge or new combinations of old knowledge are embodied in new products or processes introduced into the economy (Oerlemans, Meeus, and Boekema 1998). Therefore, innovation involves the use of existing knowledge as well as the ability to generate and acquire new knowledge

(Howells 2002). Consequently, firms increasingly rely on knowledge as a key input of successful and long-lasting innovation activities (Pinch et al. 2003). In other words, firms' sustainable competitiveness is highly dependent on their ability to innovate and, therefore, on their ability to improve their knowledge base (Cooke 2001, Florida 1995, Malmberg and Maskell 2002). Saviotti (1999) defines firm knowledge base as the collective character of the knowledge, which depends both on individual human resources and on the mechanisms of interaction within the organization (Morone and Taylor 2010).

We now turn to explore how innovation affects the way we live and produce.

2.3 THE EFFECTS OF INNOVATION: TECHNOLOGICAL CHANGE

Innovation has significant effects on the progress of our societies. There are clear effects on trade, market structures, wealth creation, competitiveness, and sustainability (Swann 2009). Innovation and technological change are highly related and some authors use them interchangeably. Nevertheless, Swann (2009) defined technological change as the process of creating and applying new technological knowledge.

Solow (1957) demonstrated the power of technological change on economic growth. He proved that productivity—measured by gross output per man-hour—doubled over the period 1909–1949, with 87.5% of the increase attributable to technical change and the remaining 12.5% to the increased use of capital. According to Nelson (1987) and Dosi (1988), technological change is the search for an increase in the known set of production processes. This implies the view that technological change is cumulative, giving rise to path dependency in the economic system. Driscoll (2014, p. 318) defines path dependency as "a self-reinforcing process by which each step along a given path increases the likelihood of further steps in the same direction." According to him, once certain thresholds are reached, the costs of reversal or path alteration become prohibitively high, leading to socio-technical and institutional lock-in. This leads to the concept of technological trajectories. A technological trajectory is defined as "the pattern of 'normal' problem solving activity on the grounds of a technological paradigm" (Dosi 1982, p. 152). Abbott (1997) suggested another way to conceptualize these notions by recasting them in terms of trajectories and turning points. Trajectories are interlocked and interdependent sequences of events, whereas turning points are events that have the potential to redirect trajectories along new paths. Trajectories have thus an inertial character, coercing processes within along predetermined paths and their ability to absorb minor variations and ruptures in processes without any appreciable impact on the overall direction of the trajectory (Sewell 1992). Araujo and Harrison (1997, p. 4) stressed that turning points are "more consequential than trajectories since they switch trajectories to new paths." This leads to the concept of clusters of innovation that help understand these turning points.

2.3.1 Clusters of Innovations and Economic Growth

Schumpeter (1939, p. 75) observed and anticipated that innovations are not evenly distributed in time but that, on the contrary, tend to cluster to come about in bunches, simply because first some and then most firms follow in the wake of successful innovations. For instance, Freeman and Soete (1997) identified some of these clusters of innovation:

- Industrial Revolution (1800s): The factory system, canal mania, mechanization of textiles, production of pig iron.
- Age of Steam and Railways (1850s): The telegraph, the rise of steam as a pervasive technology.
- Age of Electricity (1900s): Bessemer process, joint-stock company, Thomas A. Edison, the rise of electricity as pervasive technology.
- Age of Mass Production (1950s): Managerial capitalism, assembly belt, the American system of manufacturing.
- The Information Age (2000s): Networks, the rise of information and communication technology.
- Cyber-Physical Systems (2020-): Characterized by changes in velocity, scope, and systems, impacts of current breakthroughs (e.g., artificial intelligence).

However, these clusters of innovation did not happen at the same time for all countries in the world, yielding technological gaps. Differences in economic performance among countries, regions, industries, or companies can be explained by these technology gaps. Technology gap is to be understood as a disparity in the levels and rates of change of technology.

The emphasis of newer technologies requires the distinction between *technology* and high-technology. For the OECD (1986), the distinction resides in the level of research and development (R&D) achieved. Therefore, *high-tech industries* are those that spend more than 5% of their turnover into R&D (e.g., aerospace, computers, electronics, pharmaceuticals). Medium high-tech industries spend between 5% and 3%, whereas medium low-tech industries spend 3% to 0.9%, and low-tech industries between 0.9% and none of the turnover into R&D. The following typology of technology (Sharp and Pavitt 1998) helps distinguish how the technology can be or cannot be disseminated.

> *Key technology*: Specific knowledge that enables a firm to keep up with or ahead of its competitors.
> *Core technology*: A technology the mastery of which is essential to the development of an industrial sector.
> *Generic technology* or *pervasive technology*: Widespread application of technology across many sectors.
> *Strategic technology*: One that enables a nation or region to keep its economic independence.

The diffusion of these technologies among industries matters, and it should be understood as the process by which the use of an innovation spreads and grows (Mansfield et al. 1977). In this regard, the notion of National Innovation System results is important. It is "the sets of institutions within an economy whose interactions determine the level of innovative performance of national firms" (Nelson 1993). At the microeconomic level, the innovation value chain model coined by Roper et al. (2008) offers an appropriate framework to understand how the innovative process works. It is defined as the "process through which firms source the knowledge they need to undertake innovation, transform this knowledge into new products and processes, and then exploit their innovations to generate added value" (Roper et al. 2008, p. 961). This concept has proven to be helpful and adopted in further empirical researches that assessed the likelihood of innovation in global value chains (Martinez-Covarrubias et al. 2016). In this vein, Chapter 4 delves into innovation in global supply chain management. However, for now, the following chapter offers an understanding of the external determinants of innovation, economics of location, among other relevant factors, which play a critical role on the innovativeness of organizations.

2.4 SUMMARY

This chapter offered a review of the theoretical foundations to help the operations manager to grasp innovation as a concept. This review provides the foundations to delve into the following chapters. Economic theories to explain innovation were covered with particular emphasis on the evolutionary theory, which provides a consistent and robust framework to understand and acknowledge innovation as a complex and dynamic phenomenon. The effects of innovation and technological change on economic growth were explored too. A brief review on clusters of innovation, in terms of time and economic growth, helps to understand how technological change has influenced the progress of our societies.

The following chapters adopt a more practical approach. They explore how innovation processes interact with key relevant aspects such as location, global supply chain management, culture, organizational structure, new product/service and processes design, and sustainability.

KEY POINTS TO REMEMBER

- Innovation is a complex process that requires different views to be understood.
- The most appropriate theory to understand innovation is the evolutionary theory.
- The most simple and general definition of innovation is *the successful exploitation of new ideas.*
- In order to innovate, relevant prior knowledge is required—absorptive capacity.
- Absorptive capacity is defined as "...prior related knowledge which confers an ability to recognize the value of new information, assimilate it, and apply it to commercial ends" (Cohen and Levinthal 1990, p. 128).
- Types of innovation: product, process, marketing, and organizational.
- Technological change fuels economic progress. Technological change is the process of creating and applying new technological knowledge.

It is cumulative, giving rise to path dependency and technological trajectories in the economic system.

- Clusters of innovation: industrial revolution, age of steam and railways, age of electricity, age of mass production, information age, and age of cyber-physical systems.

REFERENCES

Abbott, A. 1997. On the concept of turning point. *Comparative Social Research* 16:85–106.

Andreosso, B. and D. Jacobson. 2005. *Industrial Economics and Organisation: A European Perspective*. 2nd ed. Berkshire, UK: McGraw-Hill.

Aoki, M. 1984. *The Co-operative Game Theory of the Firm*. Oxford, UK: Clarendon Press.

Araujo, L. and D. Harrison. 1997. Technological trajectories and path dependence. Available at: https://pdfs.semanticscholar.org/24c3/4a9316f780b8c0a4948962924a20300b79c1.pdf (accessed on May 03, 2017).

Audretsch, D. B. and A. R. Thurik. 2001. What's new about the new economy? Sources of growth in the managed and entrepreneurial economies. *Industrial & Corporate Change* 10(1):267–315.

Auerbach, P. 1989. *Competition: The Economics of Industrial Change*. Oxford, UK: Basil Blackwell.

Barney, J. B. 1991a. Firm resources and sustained competitive advantage. *Journal of Management* 17(1):99–121.

Barney, J. B. 1991b. The resource based view of strategy: Origins, implications, and prospects. *Journal of Management* 17:97–211.

Baumol, W. J. 1967. *Business Behaviour, Value and Growth*. New York, NY: Harcourt Brace Jovanovich.

Berle, A. A. and G. C. Means. 1932. *The Modern Corporation and Private Property*. New York, NY: Macmillan.

Chandler, A. D. 1992a. Organisational capabilities and the economic history of the industrial enterprise. *Journal of Economic Perspectives* 6(3):79–100.

Chandler, A. D. 1992b. What is a Firm? *European Economics Review* 36(2–3):483–492.

Chandler, A. D., Jr. 1990. *Scale and Scope: The Dynamics of Industrial Capitalism*. Cambridge, MA: Belknap/Harvard University Press.

Clark, N. and C. Juma. 1987. *Long Run Economics: An Evolutionary Approach to Economic Growth*. London, UK: Pinter Publishers.

Coase, R. H. 1937. The nature of the firm. *Economica* 4(16):386–405.

Cohen, W. M. and D. A. Levinthal. 1990. Absorptive capacity: A new perspective on learning and innovation. *Administrative Science Quarterly* 35(1):128–152.

Cooke, P. 2001. *Knowledge Economies: Clusters, Learning and Co-Operative Advantage*. London, UK: Routledge.

Demsetz, H. 1991. The theory of the firm revisited. In *The Nature of the Firm*, H. Demsetz (Ed.). pp. 159–178. New York, NY: Oxford University Press.

Dosi, G., R. R. Nelson, and S. G. Winter. 2001. *The Nature and Dynamics of Organizational Capabilities*. Oxford, UK: Oxford University Press.

Dosi, G. 1982. Technological paradigms and technological trajectories: A suggested interpretation of the determinants and directions of technical change. *Research Policy* 11(3):147–162.

Dosi, G. 1988. The nature of the innovation process. In *Technical Change and Economic Theory*, G. Dosi, C. Freeman, R. R. Nelson, G. Silverberg and L. Soete (Eds.). pp. 221–238. London, UK: Pinter Publishers.

Douma, S. and H. Schreuder. 1992. *Economic Approaches to Organisations*. Hertfordshire, UK: Prentice Hall.

Driscoll, P. A. 2014. Breaking carbon lock-in: Path dependencies in large-scale transportation infrastructure projects. *Planning Practice and Research* 29(3):317–330.

Fagerberg, J., D. Mowery, and R. Nelson. 2005. *The Oxford Handbook of Innovation*. Oxford, UK: Oxford University Press.

Fama, E. and M. C. Jensen. 1983. The separation of ownership and control. *Journal of Law and Economics* 26(2):301–325.

Florida, R. L. 1995. Toward the learning region. *Futures* 27(5):527–536.

Freeman, C. and L. Soete. 1997. *The Economics of Industrial Innovation*. 3rd ed. London, UK: Pinter Publishers.

Freeman, R. E. 1984. *Strategic Management: A Stakeholder Approach*. Boston, MA: Pitman.

Grant, R. M. 1996. Toward a knowledge-based theory of the firm. *Strategic Management Journal* 17:109–122.

Grant, R. M. 2006. The knowledge-based view of the firm. In *The Oxford Handbook of Strategy: A Strategy Overview and Competitive Strategy*, D. O. Faulkner and A. Campbell (Eds.). Oxford, UK: Oxford Handbooks Online.

Hodgson, G. 2002. Evolutionary theories of the firm. In *The IEBM Handbook of Economics*, W. Lazonick (Ed.). London, UK: Thomson.

Howells, J. R. L. 2002. Tacit knowledge, innovation and economic geography. *Urban Studies* 39(5–6):871–884.

Jevons, W. S. 1879. *The Theory of Political Economy*. Hampshire, UK: Macmillan.

Kogut, B. and U. Zander. 1992. Knowledge of the firm, combinative capabilities, and the replication of technology. *Organization Science* 3:383–397.

Korres, G. M. 2016. *Technical Change and Economic Growth: Inside the Knowledge Based Economy*. 2nd ed. New York, NY: Routledge.

Kuznets, S. 1973. Modern economic growth: Findings and reflections. *The American Economic Review* 63(3):247–258.

Lazonick, W. 1991. *Business Organization and the Myth of the Market Economy*. Cambridge, MA: Cambridge University Press.

Lazonick, W. 2010. The Chandlerian corporation and the theory of innovative enterprise. *Industrial and Corporate Change* 19(2):317–349.

Machlup, F. M. 1980. *Knowledge: Its Creation Distribution and Economic Significance*. Princeton, NJ: Princeton University Press.

Malmberg, A. and P. Maskell. 2002. The elusive concept of localisation economies: Towards a knowledge-based theory of spatial clustering. *Environment and Planning A* 34(3):429–449.

Mansfield, E., J. Rapoport, A. Romeo, S. Wagner, and G. Beardsley. 1977. Social and private rates of return from industrial innovations. *Quarterly Journal of Economics* 91(2):221–240.

March, J. G. and H. A. Simon. 1958. *Organization*. New York, NY: John Wiley & Sons.

Marshall, A. 1890. *Principles of Economics*. Revised Edition. London, UK: Macmillan; reprinted in 1920 by Prometheus Books.

Martinez-Covarrubias, J. L., H. Lenihan, and M. Hart. 2016. Public support for business innovation in Mexico: A cross-sectional analysis. *Regional Studies*. DOI: http://dx.doi.org/10.1080/00343404.2016.1245414.

Metcalfe, J. S. 1995. The design of order. Notes on evolutionary principles and the dynamics of innovation. *Revue Économique* 46(6):1561–1583.

Morone, P. and R. Taylor. 2010. *Knowledge Diffusion and Innovation*. Cheltenham, UK: Edward Elgar Publishing Ltd.

Nelson, R. R. 1987. Innovation and economic developments: Theoretical retrospect and prospect. In *Technology Generation in Latin American Manufacturing Industries*, J. Katz (Ed.). London, UK: Macmillan.

Nelson, R. R. and N. Rosenberg. 1993. Technical innovation and national systems. In *National Innovation Systems: A Comparative Analysis*, R. R. Nelson (Ed.). pp. 3–22. Oxford, UK: Oxford University Press.

Nelson, R. R. and S. G. Winter. 1982. *An Evolutionary Theory of Economic Change*. Cambridge, MA: Harvard University Press.

Nelson, R. R. 1993. *National Innovation Systems*. Oxford, UK: Oxford University Press.

Nelson, R. R. and S. G. Winter. 1974. Neoclassical vs. evolutionary theories of economic growth: Critique and prospectus. *Economic Journal* 84(336):886–905.

Nonaka, I. 1994. A dynamic theory of organizational knowledge creation. *Organization Science* 5:14–37.

O'Sullivan, M. 2000. *Contest for Corporate Control: Corporate Governance and Economic Performance in the United States and Germany*. Oxford, UK: Oxford University Press.

OECD. 1986. *Technical Cooperation Agreements Between Firms: Some Initial Data and Analysis*. Paris, France: OECD.

OECD. 2005. *Oslo Manual: Guidelines for Collecting and Interpreting Innovation Data*. 3rd ed., *Science & Information Technology*. Paris, France: OECD. Original edition, The Measurement of Scientific and Technological Activities Oslo Manual: Guidelines for Collecting and Interpreting Innovation Data.

Oerlemans, L., M. Meeus, and F. Boekema. 1998. Learning, Innovation and Proximity. Eindhoven Centre for Innovation Studies, the Netherlands.

Penrose, E, ed. 1959. *The Theory of the Growth of the Firm*. New York, NY: John Wiley & Sons.

Pinch, S., N. Henry, M. Jenkins, and S. Tallman. 2003. From 'industrial districts' to 'knowledge clusters': A model of knowledge dissemination and competitive advantage in industrial agglomeration. *Journal of Economic Geography* 3:373–388.

Robertson, P. L. and R. N. Langlois. 1994. Institutions, inertia and changing industrial leadership. *Industrial and Corporate Change* 3(2):359–378.

Romer, P. M. 1990. Endogenous technological change. *The Journal of Political Economy* 98(5):S71–S102.

Roper, S., J. Du, and J. Love. 2008. Modelling the innovation value chain. *Research Policy* 37(6–7):961–977.

Saviotti, P. P. 1999. Knowledge, information and organisational structures. In *Authority and Control in Modern Industry*, P. L. Robertson (Ed.). London, UK: Routledge.

Schumpeter, J. A. 1934. *The Theory of Economic Development*. Cambridge, MA: Harvard University Press.

Schumpeter, J. A. 1939. *Business Cycles: A Theoretical, Historical and Statistical Analysis, Vols. 1 and 2*. New York, NY: McGraw-Hill.

Schumpeter, J. A. 1943. *Capitalism, Socialism and Democracy*. London, UK: Allen and Unwin.

Schumpeter, J. 1928. The instability of capitalism. *The Economic Journal* 38(151):361–386.

Schumpeter, J. A. 1947. The creative response in economic history. *The Journal of Economic History* 7(2):149–159.

Sewell, W. H. 1992. A theory of structure: Duality, agency, and transformation. *American Journal of Sociology* 98(1):1–29.

Shapiro, C. and H. Varian. 1999. Information rules. *California Management Review* 41(2):8–32.

Sharp, M. and K. Pavitt. 1998. Technology policy in the 1990s. *International Economic Integration: General Issues* 3(2):262.

Simon, H. A. 1960. *The New Science of Management Decision*. New York, NY: Harper & Row.

Simon, H. A. 1991. Bounded rationality and organisational learning. *Organization Science* 2:125–134.

Solow, R. M. 1957. Technical change and the aggregate production function. *The Review of Economic and Statistics* 39:312–320.

Swann, G. M. P. 2009. *The Economics of Innovation: An Introduction*. Cheltenham, UK: Edward Elgar Publishing Ltd.

Wahid, A. N. M. 2002. *Frontiers of Economics: Nobel Laureates of the Twentieth Century*. Westport, CT: Greenwood Press.

Walras, L. 1874. *Elements of Pure Economics: Or, the Theory of Social Wealth*. Taylor & Francis. Original edition, Éléments d'économie politique pure, ou théorie de la richesse sociale.

Wernerfelt, B. 1984. A resource-based view of the firm. *Strategic Management Journal* 5:171–180.

Williamson, O. E. 1985. *The Economic Institutions of Capitalism*. New York, NY: Free Press.

Winter, G. 1995. Four Rs of profitability: Rents, resources, routines, and replication. In *Resource-Based and Evolutionary Theories of the Firm: Towards a Synthesis*, C. Montgomery (Ed.). pp. 147–177. Hingham, MA: Kluwer.

Section II

Understanding
the External Context

Section II

Understanding
the External Context

3

Location, Location, Location: External Determinants of Innovation Performance

3.1 INTRODUCTION

As discussed in previous chapters, the capacity to innovate depends upon a series of factors which can be grouped into two: (1) internal capacities, such as technological capabilities or absorptive capacity; and (2) external conditions. The latter group relates to the environment in which the company operates. Some elements of such an environment relate to the degree of market competition, geographical location, and proximity to markets, sources of information and knowledge, access to a specialized pool of skilled workers, how the business is integrated in the value chain they serve, and so on. Fagerberg et al. (2005) recognize that innovative activity is not uniformly or randomly distributed across the geographical landscape. This has important implications if an operations manager or a manager director is deciding where to establish and perform innovative activities or if there is no location decision to make as the firm is already established in a specific location—to understand that the environment where it operates would affect its capacity to innovate. This chapter goes beyond the competitive environment—discussed in previous chapters— by exploring these external factors that affect the capacity to innovate. It offers insights into operations managers with regard to the optimal location to pursue innovation. Section 3.2 presents a summary of the external determinants for innovation. Section 3.3 explores the economies of location and discusses the agglomeration effects. Section 3.4 delves into clusters. Section 3.5 examines the role of industrial policies that governments adopt to support businesses to innovate in their jurisdictions as a means to achieve the sustainable economic performance of the locality, region, or nation. Finally, Section 3.6 offers criteria to decide where to locate innovation and operations activities.

3.2 EXTERNAL DETERMINANTS FOR INNOVATION

The reader should bear in mind the external aspects that affect the capacity to innovate. These range from patterns of learning and innovation in different economic sectors, the degree of competition and market structures in inputs and outputs—as discussed in previous chapters—whether or not the firm is inserted in a global supply chain—which is further discussed in the next chapter—and agglomeration effects emerging due to proximity to a spatial concentration of businesses to name a few. The presence of these external aspects in a specific location affects the propensity of firms to innovate. A clear example of this is *Silicon Valley*, which has drawn global attention given its spectacular growth and development. Many countries and locations in the world are trying to emulate this success story. The decision by managing directors of high-tech companies such as Google and Apple to locate their headquarters and R&D facilities in the San Francisco Bay Area in California is underpinned by the availability of factors that create this location as an innovation-friendly business ecosystem. The remaining sections of this chapter will delve into how these external factors—environment in which firms operate—affect the propensity of firms to innovate. The following section in particular delves into benefits and economic advantages of locating operations and innovative activities in specific places. This is useful for operations managers to understand why firms tend to concentrate in particular locations.

3.3 ECONOMIES OF LOCATION

Traditionally, the discipline of economics has paid little attention to the location of operations as a key driver of business performance. Few researchers on the theories of the firm such as Andreosso and Jacobson (2005) have viewed geography as a fundamental element to explain the nature and performance of the firm; see Porter (1990, 1998) and Best (1990, 2001). Location theory proposes that firms locate so as to minimize costs and seek locations that maximize their opportunities to reach markets, thus to maximize profits. This is coupled with the view from Feldman (2001), Cortright, and Mayer (2002) that the more knowledge-intensive the economic activity, the more geographically clustered it tends to be. Andreosso and Jacobson (2005) stressed that the importance of location as an important factor of the organization of production can be traced back to Marshall (1890). He identified six main factors in the localization of firms and industries, which are described as follows.

3.3.1 Causes of Location Advantages

1. *Physical conditions.* These are the conditions such as climate, soil, topography, and availability and access to raw materials. For instance, an industry requiring raw materials that are expensive to transport is likely to locate near the source of those materials.
2. *Demand conditions.* Products tend to be produced close to their market to minimize costs of transportation. A high-income market may generate a demand for high-quality goods, attracting a skilled workforce, and educates those on the spot.
3. *Political/cultural influences.* According to Marshall, "the character of the people, and their social and political institutions," and to individuals' "ideals of life" determine how they exploit natural advantages.

3.3.2 Location Advantages

4. *Hereditary skill.* This is the situation in which a large number of people lived and worked—using similar, specialized skills—in close proximity. The skills in the production of the particular product become so well known in the area that *children learn many of them unconsciously.* Inventions and improvements in machinery, in process, and in the general organization of the business become quickly known and copied. This is referred to as technological spillovers (Krugman 1993), that is, "the more or less pure externality that results from knowledge spillovers between nearby firms."
5. *The growth of subsidiary trades.* The location of an industry attracts firms that supply intermediate goods, including manufacturing

equipment, to that industry. Krugman (1993) argued that the concentration of suppliers of intermediate goods in the same location as their customers "depend crucially on at least some degree of economies of scale... it is only the presence of increasing returns that makes a large centre of production able to have more efficient and more diverse suppliers than a small one." This should be considered in tandem with economies of scope, when different types of products are produced in the same production line creating costs savings.

6. *Local market for special skills required by the industry.* A localized industry *gains a greater advantage from the fact that it offers a constant market for skill.* The interests of workers with these skills and their employers are mutually reinforced by location. Employers will tend to locate where the skill is available, and those with the skill will tend to live where employers of the skill are concentrated: *social forces here cooperate with economic forces.* Workers follow jobs and jobs follow workers.

These factors help understand the agglomeration effects or economies that firms may enjoy.

3.3.3 Agglomeration Economies

From Marshall's six localization factors and under certain circumstances, firms within an industry or in related industries will agglomerate. They will locate close to each other. Agglomeration economies will be greater than the benefits that firms derive from a more diffuse location.

Agglomeration effects explain why some regions develop large concentrations or clusters of certain types of economic activities (Swann 2009). A lot of work on agglomeration economies stems from the concept of the industrial district proposed by Alfred Marshall (1890). These agglomeration effects are benefits available to individuals and firms in large concentrations of population and economic activity. Agglomeration effects refer to economies of scale, that is, the factors that make it possible for large organizations or regions to produce goods and services more cheaply than smaller ones. These agglomeration effects also refer to economies of scope that arise through the opportunities of large concentrations of population and activity, which provide for diversified activities to occur through linkages among firms of various sizes. Externality effects arise too. They relate to the advantages gained through proximity to diversified business and market opportunities as a result of the concentration of people and activities in particular locations. This leads to the concept of knowledge spillovers. These are defined as "…intellectual gains through exchange of information for which a direct compensation for the producer of the knowledge is not given, or for which less compensation is given than the value of the knowledge" (Jaffe 1996, p. 5).

Agglomeration economies can be used to distinguish between *mere* spatial concentration and a *proper* industrial agglomeration (Heanue and Jacobson 2001). Agglomeration economies are benefits that a firm derives from the fact that there are other firms located in the same place. They are a subset of Marshall's external economies described previously. An industrial agglomeration is thus a spatial concentration of firms where the motivations for, and results of, being spatially concentrated are that the individual firms are in some economic sense better off that they would have been if they were located in an industrially more isolated and scattered setting.

It is important to distinguish between mere *concentrations* from *agglomerations*. On the one hand, even if agglomeration economies were not the initial driver of the spatial concentration, that concentration may still lead to what Weber (1909) called *accidental agglomeration economies*. On the other hand, such spatial concentrations may not lead to agglomeration economies, in which case, it should not be called an *agglomeration*, but instead *concentration*. For example, where a number of firms concentrate in a particular place because of a government incentive to do so but there is no gain from the fact that there are other firms in that place—such as external economies or economies of scope—such spatial grouping constitutes a concentration but not an agglomeration.

Now the chapter turns to delve into what a cluster of firms entails.

3.4 CLUSTERS

Although there is an extensive debate on the typologies of industrial agglomerations such as industrial districts, filieres, clusters, and regional innovation systems (see Andreosso and Jacobson 2005), this chapter particularly focuses on clusters given the mainstream use of this concept, and therefore we offer a special attention. A cluster comprises of direct and indirect relationships that compete with each other and cooperate with each other in an industry involved in a specific product category. The cluster is a broader concept, including firms on different product categories, though this may depend on how the term *product category* is defined. The World Bank offers a short definition for cluster: "An agglomeration of companies, suppliers, service providers, and associated institutions in a particular field" (WB 2009, p. 1).

However, definitions as to what exactly constitutes a cluster vary greatly. Möhring (2005, p. 21) defines clustering as "local concentrations of horizontally or vertically linked firms that specialise in related lines of business together with supporting organisations." On this line of thought, firms can achieve economies of scale and scope and lower their transaction costs by clustering together. Business clustering refers to geographical concentrations of horizontally or vertically linked firms that specialize in related lines of business together with supporting organizations. Also, clusters allow firms to thrive under conditions of increasing global competition. Clusters have been identified as motors for innovation. Competition, as well as by the possibility of cost-sharing among cluster participants, enables the introduction of new technologies. Firms competing and cooperating at close proximity can learn from each other developing unique local knowledge and spurring knowledge spillovers. Clusters vary widely regarding the number of participants and their degree of organization. Clustering occurs in all branches of industry, from high-tech to traditional industries, from agriculture to the service sector, with each cluster being a unique constellation in time and space.

Nevertheless, the reader should bear in mind that the cluster concept has attracted criticism (Martin and Sunley 2003). There is overemphasis placed on cooperation and exclusion of negative aspects of clusters, such as power asymmetries in supply chains where larger firms often dictate terms of collaboration. Methodologies used to identify clusters are often crude. They rely solely on measuring industry concentrations overlooking that collocation does not always result in clustering. Another criticism is that policy makers stand accused of identifying more clusters than actually exist. Too much emphasis is often put on small- and medium-sized enterprises (SMEs) and bottom-up approaches, neglecting the role that large firms and governments play (Markusen 1996). In a similar vein, cluster policy lacks foundations given the fact that clusters are supposed to emerge spontaneously and, therefore, presumably cannot be created simply by policy intervention. Critics emphasize that clusters are no panacea for economic development, as in fact clusters can help only a few firms in selected areas. Despite this criticism, cluster policy is still employed by most governments in the world aiming at creating an innovation-friendly ecosystem.

Different typologies and methods regarding the analysis of clusters have emerged. For instance, Markusen (1996) stressed the role of large multinational firms and governments at the national and regional levels. Some models to represent clusters refer to *Hub and Spoke District*, the *Satellite Industrial Platform*, and the *State-centered District*, to name a few. By measuring regional competitiveness, Porter (2003) identifies the following types of industrial clusters: resource-dependent, local, and traded. In terms of cluster-development stages, Enright (2000) proposes a cluster classification differentiating between working clusters, latent clusters, potential clusters, policy-driven clusters, and wishful-thinking clusters.

Since there are different cluster typologies, different theories are required to explain how they operate. Additionally, different methods of measurement are required so that policy makers can measure the performance of clusters (Möhring 2005). Although there is no uniform universal definition as to what exactly a cluster constitutes, the literature on clusters (Enright 2000, Markusen 1996, Porter 2003), however, recognizes the essence of this phenomenon: clusters occur due to proximity to markets, the presence of specialized labor, the availability of infrastructure, as well as other inputs such as natural resources, information, equipment/service suppliers, and so on.

Swann (2009, pp. 149–150) offers a very simple way to grasp the concept of cluster and its degree of measurement. Table 3.1 summarizes the framework as a simple one-dimensional spectrum of interpretation, from shallow to rich.

At the top of the table, the shallowest definition of clustering simply says that a group of firms are co-located. A slightly more demanding definition is that this co-located group should also be technologically related (e.g., they are in the same industry sector, as in Silicon Valley). The next step downward would require that these co-located firms should show superior performance and that this is attributable to their location in a cluster (i.e., displaying economies of agglomeration). A next step would be that these firms in the cluster are explicitly interrelated in a value chain. The next step down the ladder is that firms in the cluster have an explicit strategy as *network firms* and exploit

TABLE 3.1

Theoretical Definition of a Cluster: Variations on the Cluster Concept

Phenomenon	Difficulty of Measurement	Richness of Cluster
Co-location	Easy	Shallow
Co-location and technological proximity		
Co-location and superior performance		
Companies interdependent in a value chain		
Network firms		
Marshallian externalities		
Labor mobility		
Explicit collaboration		
Informal knowledge exchange	Difficult	Rich

Source: Adapted from Swann, G. M. P. *The Economics of Innovation: An Introduction,* Edward Elgar Publishing Ltd., Cheltenham, UK, 2009.

the existence of all the other network firms in the cluster. Network firms are firms that specialize in a very narrow part of the vertical chain and outsource most other activities. Such network firms are common in strong industrial clusters and benefit from location in strong clusters (networks) when: (a) the required competences are uncommon and no team member has them all and (b) the ability of team members to work with each other cannot be taken for granted, so it helps to have a large pool to draw on.

The next step down is that firms in the cluster enjoy the sorts of mutual benefits from each other's company (i.e., Marshallian externalities that is sharing a common infrastructure, access to a pool of skilled labor, and so on). A further step down would be that there is labor mobility around this network, and this is important because mobile labor is one of the most effective ways of transferring technology around all the firms in a cluster. A further step down would be that companies in the cluster have explicit collaboration in R&D—without falling into antitrust behavior. And the final step is knowledge spillovers, that is, the sort of informal knowledge exchange between technologists of different, even rival companies in informal, social, and casual meetings (such as those at the bar after work).

It is important stressing that the phenomenon at the top of Table 3.1 is relatively easy to measure, and as one goes down the ladder, the measurement of such phenomenon becomes more challenging.

The chapter now turns to offer views of why governments formulate policies to create an innovation-friendly ecosystem environment to attract investment to their jurisdictions.

3.5 ROLE OF GOVERNMENTS IN SUPPORTING INNOVATION: INDUSTRIAL POLICY

When deciding where to locate an R&D laboratory, or where to carry out research, development, and innovations, the reader should bear in mind the actions carried out by governments to reinforce the decision with incentives to locate in their jurisdictions. Alternatively, if you are already located, this section may provide you with insights about what you are missing or what you can demand from your local authority. If you are a local government official, the following may shed some light on to what you can do to spur innovation in your locality. You can realize this opportunity that can give you an edge.

Some innovation policy instruments available to firms wishing to locate in a particular location, or already located are as follows:

- *R&D subsidies* (grants). In 2012, the 8% of the UK Business Expenditure in R&D (BERD) was funded by direct grants from government (£1.3 billion).
- *R&D tax credits.* Another similar 8% of UK BERD was funded through tax credits (£1.4 billion).
- *Corporation tax: R&D tax relief.*[*] Ireland offers an attractive corporate tax regime for companies looking to locate businesses in the country.[†]
- *Grants* for filling *patent* applications.
- *Grants* for operation of *business networks* (e.g., chamber of commerce).
- *Innovation vouchers.* For instance, Ireland offers these instruments (worth €5,000) to build links between Ireland's public knowledge providers (i.e., higher education institutes, public research bodies) and small businesses.

---

[*] https://www.gov.uk/guidance/corporation-tax-research-and-development-rd-relief
[†] http://www.idaireland.com/invest-in-ireland/ireland-corporate-tax/

These instruments and the magnitude of their support differ from country to country. For a more up-to-date information on the range of instruments provided by different countries, the reader should refer to the Global Observatory of Science, Technology and Innovation Policy Instruments (GO-SPIN*). This observatory provides key information on science, technology, and innovation (STI) governing bodies, legal frameworks, policy instruments, and long-term series of indicators for evidence-based policy analysis, design, and foresight studies.

The chapter now turns to offer location criteria—based on a review of the literature of clusters for R&D—for deciding where to establish your R&D and innovation activities. If you are already established in a particular location, then the same criteria can assist you to assess whether or not you are placed in a prone innovation environment or if you are missing something to your benefit.

―――――――――

3.6 HOW TO DECIDE WHERE TO LOCATE MY INNOVATION AND OPERATIONS ACTIVITIES?

The company's location decision for its operations and innovation activities, like many other economic decisions, is one where there is some element of choice at an initial stage, but by the time the company is firmly established in a particular location, it is much less likely to move—even if there would be some benefits in doing so. Therefore, first we need to address two questions: (1) Why do companies making location decisions tend to cluster? and (2) why do well-established companies tend to stay where they are? The first is more interesting one. In general, these decisions are taken when advantages outweigh disadvantages. The second is often a case of a lock-in. It would be too expensive to relocate, so that any benefits from relocation are outweighed by switching costs (Swann 2009).

Companies making location decisions rely on a variety of reasons. The benefits from clustering can be grouped into two types: demand side and supply side. The reader should note that along advantages, there can also be disadvantages, and these too can also be broken into demand side and

―――――――――

* http://en.unesco.org/go-spin GO-SPIN is an online, open access platform for decision-makers, knowledge- brokers, specialists and general-public, with a wide range of information on STI policies

TABLE 3.2

Advantages and Disadvantages of Clustering

	Advantages	Disadvantages
Demand Side	• Strong local customers (test bed) • Reduced customer search costs • Market share gains from clustering • Information externalities • Reduced transaction costs	• Competition in output markets
Supply Side	• Strong local suppliers • Pool of specialized labor and other specialized inputs • Shared infrastructure • Reduced transaction costs • Information externalities and knowledge spillovers • Facilitates innovation	• Competition in input markets (real state, labor)—*overheating* • Local infrastructure over-stretched • Congestion (e.g., in transportation) • Cartels • *New ideas need new space*

Source: Adapted from Swann, G. M. P. *The Economics of Innovation: An Introduction*, Edward Elgar Publishing Ltd., Cheltenham, UK, 2009.

supply side disadvantages. Invoking Swann (2009), the following advantages and disadvantages are presented as a criterion to decide where to locate innovation and operations activities (Table 3.2).

3.6.1 Advantages on the Demand Side

3.6.1.1 *Strong Local Customers (Test Bed)*

Some companies benefit from having strong local customers for their products and services. In an age of low transportation costs and online services, this may seem surprising. The existence and strength of local customers might not appear to matter very much. But companies benefit enormously from close contact with their active consumers, because active consumers are often an important source of ideas for the next generation of innovative products.

3.6.1.2 *Reduced Customer Search Costs*

Companies may benefit from location in a cluster because that reduces the search costs of potential customers. Location in a cluster means that the discerning consumer will be more likely to search my store to see if he or she can find what he or she wants. Location outside the cluster means that the customer is much less likely to find what I have in store.

3.6.1.3 Market Share Gains from Clustering

This is the idea captured in Hotellings (1929) famous old model of the two ice-cream sellers located on a beach. In certain conditions, the model shows that the equilibrium outcome is for the two sellers to cluster together side by side at the middle point of the beach.

3.6.1.4 Information Externalities

The idea is that, if I see another trader selling successfully at a particular location, then that would suggest something about the strength of local demand. The other trader's visible success is creating an information externality.

3.6.1.5 Reduced Transaction Costs

Finally, clustering can reduce transaction costs more generally. Transaction costs may be important when: it is a difficult task to ensure that components from an external supplier will exactly meet the customer's requirements, it is costly to communicate with outside companies, and the customer is concerned about the risk of opportunistic behavior by subcontractors. These concerns and costs may be reduced when both parties to the transaction are located in a cluster.

The section now turns to the advantages of clustering that derive from the supply side.

3.6.2 Advantages on the Supply Side

3.6.2.1 Strong Local Suppliers

The first benefit is the existence of strong local suppliers. As presented before, in an age of low transportation costs and online services, many companies buy their inputs from global markets and their suppliers are spread over the world. But when the company is an active customer for nonstandardized components, then it may require regular face-to-face contact with its suppliers. That is easier if they are co-located in the same cluster.

3.6.2.2 Pool of Specialized Labor and Other Specialized Inputs

This is when the company has access to a large common pool of specialized labor and other specialized inputs. If the company is a very specialized requirement, then it will be more likely to find this in a large cluster than in an outpost of the industry. A specialized worker, whose services demand is limited, will generally find it most efficient to locate in a cluster because that is where the jobs will be. This is both demand-side and supply-side advantages of clustering.

3.6.2.3 Shared Infrastructure

This relates to the fact that clustered companies can share a common infrastructure which is not available to companies outside the cluster. This shared infrastructure could be very wide in scope, including transport infrastructure, public assets—such as science base and other publicly provided business services—and suitable office buildings. Many companies highlight logistics as an important reason for location in a cluster, even if they do not enjoy any of the other benefits from clustering.

3.6.2.4 Reduced Transaction Costs

Transaction with a neighboring supplier may be easier than transactions with a distant supplier. The argument here is just the same as the demand-side benefits.

3.6.2.5 Information Externalities and Knowledge Spillovers

Companies may learn from informal knowledge exchange with their neighbor suppliers just as they learn from informal knowledge exchange with their neighboring customers.

3.6.2.6 Facilitates Innovation

It has been well documented that the customer–supplier interaction plays an important role in the innovation process. In the combinatorial theory of creativity, creativity requires the inventor to bring distinct insights together. While this does not need the involvement of social networking between distinct people, it often does. Such creativity involves bringing together exactly the right mix of people with distinct but complementary expertise. The creative work is easier to achieve in a cluster with a wide diversity of participants. A common understanding is often facilitated when different groups meet face to face on a regular basis. This is easier to achieve in a cluster than at a distance.

3.6.3 Disadvantages on the Demand Side

Clustering can bring some disadvantages to the clustered firm too.

3.6.3.1 Competition in Output Markets

The clustered firm may encounter considerable competition in the local markets it supplies than it would if it were located outside a cluster. This argument is highly relevant when the main customers are local. Customers benefit through lower prices when there are a lot of competitors in a cluster, but suppliers suffer because they can only charge lower prices.

3.6.4 Disadvantages on the Supply Side

Most of the disadvantages of clustering apply to the supply side.

3.6.4.1 Competition in Input Markets (Real State, Labor)—"Overheating"

Clustered firms may face more competition in their input markets. The most obvious examples of this are the greater competition for real estate and skilled labor in a cluster. This is informally called *overheating*. For instance, financial services companies located in the City of London financial district face very high rents for their offices. This is certainly a disadvantage to locating in that cluster and is a factor in the de-clustering of some parts of the value chain.

3.6.4.2 Local Infrastructure Overstretched

In a strong and mature cluster, the local infrastructure may show signs of being overstretched. The City of London again provides a striking example of this. Sections of the London Underground date to the nineteenth century, and they were not designed to deal with the volume of passengers that now use that system.

3.6.4.3 Congestion (e.g., in Transportation)

This is a problem that many people living in major world cities complain about. Moreover, the road infrastructure around major clusters tends to become seriously congested as the cluster grows.

3.6.4.4 Cartels

The clustered firm may suffer from existing supply-side cartels. Similar to the fact that geographical proximity makes it easier for companies to collaborate in research, development and innovation, so it makes it easier for companies or other agencies to collude in their supply of critical inputs as entry barriers to newcomers.

3.6.4.5 "New Ideas Need New Space"

Invoking the autonomous theory of creativity, creativity means breaking the rules and those who do that will usually encounter resistance from their peers. As peer-group contact is much more vigorous in a cluster than outside a cluster, it may be easier to break the rules in isolation.

3.6.5 Cluster Life Cycle

The advantages and disadvantages from clustering tend to occur at different stages of the life cycle of the cluster—*fledging, taking off, approaching peak entry,* and *maturity* (Swann 2009). At the *taking off* stage, the cluster achieves a critical mass—the optimal size of a cluster where advantages start to outweigh the disadvantages. As the cluster grows, it will reach maturity, when the disadvantages of clustering are starting to catch up with the advantages. *Overheating* and congestion emerge in clusters, making mature clusters less attractive places to locate because of the rise of certain firms of cartel behavior and because the environment is not conductive to more radical innovation.

3.6.6 A Practical Check List

Table 3.3 offers to operations managers a useful screening checklist to assess whether or not a location facilitates R&D and innovation. It aims to help you on the decision to locate or maintain (or relocate) your research and innovation activities in particular places.

TABLE 3.3

Screening Checklist to Assess Whether or Not a Location Facilitates R&D and Innovation

Yes	No	Item
		Strong and active local customers (test bed)
		Strong and active local suppliers
		Reduced search costs for customers
		Reduced transaction costs with consumers and local suppliers
		Potential market share gains from clustering
		Information externalities and knowledge spillovers (e.g., conferences, business association meetings, community, and social events facilitating the informal exchange of information)
		Pool of specialized labor and other specialized inputs (e.g., guilds, associations, higher education organizations)
		Available shared infrastructure
		Facilitates innovation: strong collaboration (R&D linkages), Chamber of Commerce, active business networks
		Low degree of competition in output markets
		No *overheating*: low competition in input markets (real state, labor)
		Local infrastructure not *overstretched*
		No congestion (e.g., in transportation)
		R&D collaboration instead of collusion (no cartels)
		New ideas still merging in same space (no need for *new ideas need new space*)
		Are there incentives from local authorities to establish operations? (e.g., R&D subsidies, R&D tax relief, grants for filling patent applications, innovation vouchers)
		Identifying stage of cluster's life cycle
		Incumbent firms enjoy greater advantages vis-à-vis disadvantages?
		Are incumbent firms growing faster than the industry average?
		Is the rate of start-ups increasing or decreasing?
		Is there a major university attracting high-tech industries?
		Is regional/local business expenditure in R&D (BERD) higher than the national average?
		Is the patent office (USA, EU, Japan) receiving a large amount of applications (higher than national average) from the particular location?

Source: Martinez-Covarrubias, J. L. et al. *Regional Studies*, 1–15, 2016.

For a particular location, if most of these items are present, then it is an indication of an innovation-friendly ecosystem of innovation, and locating your R&D and innovation activities in this location will bring you greater benefits to your company. This screening checklist is indicative.

3.7 SUMMARY

The capacity to innovate depends upon a series of factors that can be grouped into internal and external to the firm. This chapter dealt with the latter group as to inform the operations managers with theoretical underpinnings and insights about how the location aspect affects their prospects of innovation. Agglomeration effects are at the core of the analysis with a clear distinction between the causes of location advantages and the advantages *per se*. Particular focus was paid to the concept of clusters. Borrowing from Swann (2009), a framework was presented to facilitate our understanding of the concept of a cluster. A brief discussion of government's industrial policies toward innovation was presented in order to provide hints to the operations managers of potential available supports that governments provide. This is something you should explore in your local enterprise public office, as there may be many opportunities you could be missing. The chapter ends with a list of potential advantages and disadvantages of clustering in order to support your decision as to locate your future operations and innovation activities, or, if you are already established in a specific location, to assess if you should continue there or move to another innovation-friendly environment with greater prospects to your firm. Table 3.3 offers a simple but meaningful screening checklist to assess whether or not a location facilitates R&D and innovation. After discussing the location effects on the capacity to innovate, the following chapter delves into how global supply chain management affects or enhances innovation.

KEY POINTS TO REMEMBER

- Innovation capacity is affected by internal and external factors of the firm.
- Some of the latter factors are: patterns of learning and innovation in different economic sectors, the degree of competition and market structures in inputs and outputs markets, whether or not the firm is inserted in a global supply chain and agglomeration effects emerging by proximity to a spatial concentration of businesses.

- Agglomeration effects refer to economies of scale, that is, the factors that make it possible for large organizations or regions to produce goods and services more cheaply than smaller ones.
- World Bank offers a short definition for cluster: "An agglomeration of companies, suppliers, service providers, and associated institutions in a particular field," but the cluster definition/interpretation may differ.
- Governments formulate and implement innovation policies to make places more attractive to firms to innovate.
- Some policy instruments are R&D subsidies, R&D tax credits, grants for filling patent applications, operation of business networks, or innovation vouchers. Get access to your local government enterprise support office to see what they can offer you.
- Decisions to locate innovation activities depend upon advantages and disadvantages from the supply and demand sides, and the life-cycle stage of the cluster you are intending to establish your operations and innovation activities or you are already operating.

REFERENCES

Andreosso, B. and D. Jacobson. 2005. *Industrial Economics and Organisation: A European Perspective*. 2nd ed. Berkshire, UK: McGraw-Hill.

Best, M. 2001. *The New Competitive Advantage: The Renewal of American Industry*. Oxford, UK: Oxford University Press.

Best, M. H. 1990. *The New Competition*. Cambridge, MA: Polity Press.

Cortright, J. and H. Mayer. 2002. Report—Signs of life: The growth of biotechnology centers in the US. Washington, DC: The Brookings Institution.

Enright, J. M. 2000. The globalisation of competition and the localisation of competitive advantage: Policies towards regional clustering. In *The Globalization of Multinational Enterprise Activity and Economic Development*, N. Hood and S. Young (Eds.). pp. 303–331. Hampshire, UK: Macmillan.

Fagerberg, J., D. Mowery, and R. Nelson. 2005. *The Oxford Handbook of Innovation*. Oxford, UK: Oxford University Press.

Feldman, M. P. 2001. Where science comes to life: university bioscience, commercial spin-offs, and regional economic development. *Journal of Comparative Policy Analysis: Research and Practice* 2:345–361.

Heanue, K. and D. Jacobson. 2001. Organizational proximity and institutional learning: The evolution of a spatially dispersed network in the Irish furniture industry. *International Studies of Management & Organization* 31(4):56–72.

Hotelling, H. 1929. Stability in competition. *Economic Journal* 39(1):41–57.

Jaffe, A. B. 1996. Economic analysis of research spillovers: Implications for the advanced technology program. Economic assessment office, the advanced technology program, national institutes of standards and technology, US Department of Commerce.

Krugman, P. 1993. The current case for industrial policy. In *Protectionism and World Welfare*, D. Salvatore (Ed.). pp. 160–179. Cambridge: Cambridge University Press.

Markusen, A. 1996. Sticky places in slippery space: A typology of industrial districts. *Economic Geography* 72:293–313.

Marshall, A. 1890. *Principles of Economics*. Revised Edition. London, UK: Macmillan; reprinted in 1920 by Prometheus Books.

Martin, R. and P. Sunley. 2003. Deconstructing clusters: Chaotic concept or policy panacea? *Journal of Economic Geography* 3:5–35.

Martinez-Covarrubias, J. L., H. Lenihan, and M. Hart. 2016. Public support for business innovation in Mexico: A cross-sectional analysis. *Regional Studies* 1–15.

Möhring, J. 2005. Clusters: Definition and methodology. In *Business Clusters: Promoting Enterprise in Central and Eastern Europe*, OECD (Ed.). Paris, France: OECD Publishing.

Porter, M. 1990. *The Competitive Advantage of Nations*. New York, NY: Macmillan.

Porter, M. 1998. *Clusters and Competition: New Agendas for Companies, Governments, and Institutions*. Boston, MA: HBS Press. 197–198.

Porter, M. 2003. The economic performance of regions. *Regional Studies* 37(6–7):549–578.

Swann, G. M. P. 2009. *The Economics of Innovation: An Introduction*. Cheltenham, UK: Edward Elgar Publishing Ltd.

WB. 2009. *Clusters for Competitiveness: A Practical Guide & Policy Implications for Developing Cluster Initiatives*. Washington, DC: The World Bank.

Weber, A. 1909. *Theory of the Location of Industries*. Chicago, IL: University of Chicago Press.

4

Innovation in Global Supply Chain Management

4.1 INTRODUCTION

In today's market, globalization or internationalization is not new to any businesses, and in practice, they involve some dimension of it in their supply chains. For some, their supply chains have been significantly restructured over time as a result of globalization. It has become a norm for consideration in designing and managing today's supply chains. Over the last two decades or so, we have observed supply chains becoming more and more complex, leading to great challenges faced by businesses to address the trend of globalization. At the same time, we also see opportunities arose as a result of globalization practices and how companies have achieved their competitive advantage in their respective markets. Innovative thinking, leading to innovative approaches, will play a key role in achieving efficient and cost-effective global supply chain management.

Having already discussed the economics of innovation and defined the external determinants of innovation performance as well as the link between innovation and operations management at an organizational level, this chapter examines the impact of globalization to supply chains, which begins with some background to set the scene. The challenges and opportunities brought by globalization from the supply chain's perspective will also be discussed. The role of innovation as a key enabler to address those challenges and crystallize the opportunities will also be discussed. This chapter ends with a summary, along with key points to ponder and take on with the *globalization's hat* on and a case study illustrating innovation in global supply chain management. The chapter, therefore, provides operations managers with a clearer direction how being innovative can lead to greater improvement, which was previously not explored, in global supply chain management.

4.2 THE IMPACT OF GLOBALIZATION TO SUPPLY CHAINS

A typical supply chain refers to a network of organizations (including suppliers, manufacturers, warehouses/distribution centres, and retailers) providing a series of value-added activities to transform raw materials into finished products and deliver for consumption. This is often referred to as a multitier supply chain system. End-to-end supply chain is rather complex and segregated, and it involves various ownerships. Improving the efficiency of managing the supply chains at this magnitude would require a thorough analysis, planning, and design, which is a challenging task in practice. Various factors and considerations would need to be taken into account to achieve efficient and cost-effective supply chain management.

We have seen a wide range of techniques and tools implemented over the years to improve and manage the supply chains. This includes operational techniques, such as the Lean principle's 5s, mistake proofing Poka-Yoke, value stream mapping, and more technological-driven tools, for example, electronic data interchange (EDI), warehouse management system (WMS), and radio-frequency identification (RFID) technology. In Chapter 10, we discuss some of the most commonly used improvement strategies and techniques used by operations managers to enhance the performance of their supply chains and operations of their organizations.

Globalization, which refers to businesses operating on an international scale, has taken place in the last two decades or so and has brought different dimensions in managing supply chains. There are great implications for operations managers, and their organizations, to this shift of business practices. Given that the supply chain has been extended to a global scale, the existing complexity and challenges of managing supply chain have also been amplified as a result.

The drivers of globalization are obvious, reported as accessing low-cost economies and emerging markets, achieving economies of scale, broadening supplier and customer base with geographical diversification, reducing direct/indirect costs, accessing to advanced technology, inspiring new products/ideas, reducing market uncertainty, enhancing sustainability practice, and ultimately increasing revenue (Bowersox, et al. 2012; Burt, et al. 2010; Grant, 2006). Each of these drivers has a different level of impact on organizations and how operations managers manage and improve their operations. Given this clear competitiveness, organizations have expanded globally outside their comfort zone to address these opportunities.

Burt et al. (2010) analyzed the evolution of a global supply chain in three stages. In the first stage, organizations explore in international purchase to leverage the demand of large volumes, and hence prices could be reduced. The second stage refers to global sourcing which focuses on sourcing offshore to leverage supplier capability and to support production strategies, while the third stage involves a more holistic, global supply chain practice, optimizing supply chain networks with established supplier/customer partnership worldwide to take advantage of all dimensions of globalization. This includes moving production facilities offshore to take the full advantages of low cost and emerging market.

From the supply chain's perspective, Bowersox et al. (2012) pointed out four globalization characteristics, namely, the distance of order-to-delivery operations, documentation of transactions across businesses, diversity in work practices, and cultural variation of product demands. Simchi-Levi et al. (2009) highlighted the issues of globalization, exploring the implications of international versus regional products, local autonomy versus central control, performance expectation and evaluation information system availability, cultural and infrastructure differences, and human resource. To take the maximum advantage of globalization, operations managers need a robust, integrated strategy to efficiently manage global supply chains, supporting different operations settings in relation to national, political, and economic conditions.

The impact of globalization is vast from different dimensions of analysis. Particularly for the target readers of this book, the impact of globalization will be scrutinized at a more operational level in connection with planning and designing the supply chains. It can be seen that some impacts are inter-related and subjected to chain effects.

Longer lead time. As the supply chains have expanded globally, one should expect that the lead time of bringing products to market would be longer than if the operations are taking place regionally or nationally. These operations include sourcing, manufacturing, transporting, storage, and distribution. Therefore, market responsiveness could be compromised. Careful and thorough planning of operations and contingency is crucial to ensure that the longer lead time will not affect the business performance as a whole.

Higher risk of disruption. Given the longer supply chain with more business partners, and involving multiple modes of transportation, it exposes to a higher risk of disruption in the chain of global (especially offshore) operations, such as the shortage of materials, production stoppage, breakdown of transportation. This disruption could be a result of, for example, political instability, natural disasters, social and labor issues, communication breakdown, and unreliable suppliers. This would be the causes of unprecedented longer lead time, leading to customer demands not being fulfilled.

Additional inventories. One possible strategy that operations managers can deploy to overcome the potential disruption is to increase additional inventories to cope with unforeseen circumstances in the extended supply chains. This, obviously, will increase the holding cost and others associated with it. This strategy needs to be carefully planned not to compromise the cost advantage of globalization practice.

Limited visibility of operations. In this extended supply chain with multiple (international) players, the visibility of operations will be an issue, which is due to, for example, existing IT infrastructure, incompatible legacy system across organizations/regions, work practices, and culture. This will hinder the capability and responsiveness of company coping with unforeseen incidents in the supply chain.

Quality issues. Although one of the driving forces of globalization is cost advantage, the quality of products shall not be compromised. In the global business environment, offshore suppliers or production will be part of the extended chains, and, therefore, the quality of products and services has become harder to control.

Supplier issues. Offshore suppliers could be an issue in terms of the reliability of providing materials on time, at the right quality, and with the exact specification, which is due to different market expectation, culture, and work practice. Thus, it is crucial to have an effective supplier assessment and selection exercise to ensure that these issues are minimized.

Higher overall cost. As much as the driver to lower the overall cost is going global, there is also a possibility that the overall cost will be unexpectedly higher than thought due to the adverse impact as mentioned earlier.

It is, therefore, crucial to thoroughly assess, design, and manage the global operations, taking an innovative approach to address the opportunities in this extended supply chain, which will be discussed in the following sections.

4.3 CHALLENGES AND OPPORTUNITIES IN GLOBAL SUPPLY CHAIN MANAGEMENT

What factors lead to the challenges in managing global supply chains? Operations managers examine these factors based on PEST analysis (Political, Economic, Social, and Technological), which is a popular management tool used for macro-environmental influences (Ritson, 2008). This could be extended to consider the legal and environmental aspects—PESTEL or PESTLE. Murphy and Knemeyer (2015) and Grant et al. (2006) have discussed their views on the elements leading to these challenges.

Murphy and Knemeyer (2015) viewed them as six uncontrollable macro-environmental forces and conditions, namely, cultural, demographic, economic, natural, political, and technological. To focus on the scope of their book, they discussed the factors from the perspectives of politics, economics, and culture. Similarly, Grant et al. (2006) also explained their views on the uncontrollable elements to include political and legal, economic, competition, technology, geography, social, and cultural aspects.

It is essential for operations managers to fully understand the implications of the above-mentioned factors when doing business on an international scale or performing operations offshore. For instance, the political factor will lead to different regulations and policies on certain business functions, cultural issues will associate with the way people work and practices, and social issues may lead to practicing child labor, which is a serious crime in some countries. This comes to the term *opacity* that relates to the risks of conducting business in different countries, which is typically beyond the control of any organization (Lipsey, 2001). The opacity index was developed to assess the risk costs associated with, for example, the corruption of government, legal system, economic and enforcement policies, accounting standards, and business regulations. Developing countries tend to have a higher opacity index than developed countries due to the less transparent business functions and procedures. Lipsey (2001) has provided a list of countries with this index based on the research conducted by PricewaterhouseCoopers.

The above-mentioned factors lead to a variety of risks. Simchi-Levi et al. (2009) discussed these risks from controllable (such as forecasting accuracy and execution problems) to uncontrollable (e.g., natural disasters and epidemics), and from known–unknown to unknown–unknown which is most difficult to predict and control in managing global supply chains.

For the readers of this book, we focus on the operational aspect of challenges in managing efficient global supply chains. In general, businesses will not drift away far from the challenges of reducing costs, reducing time to market, increasing quality, and so on, and ultimately, offering the highest level of customer service!

To discuss the operational challenges in a more structured manner that operations managers and their organizations may face due to the globalization of supply chains, we will employ Slack et al.'s (2016) five operational measurements of performance. These will be discussed later within the globalization context. Figure 4.1 illustrates the five areas of operational challenges in the global supply chain context, incorporating some globalization-related factors, selected from those discussed in Neely (2011).

Cost. Quite often cost is the key driver for globalization, driving the sourcing cost down with cheaper materials offshore and cheaper production cost with lower labor cost in developing economies. However, global supply chain operations will normally incur higher transportation cost and other costs associated with international logistics operations. Thus, it is crucial for operations managers to perform a thorough total cost analysis to assess direct and indirect costs to ensure that the competitiveness of global supply chains is fully realized. In recent years, the above-mentioned costs have increased in the desired emerging countries, but other driving

FIGURE 4.1
Five challenges in global supply chain context.

forces, such as local market share, have taken precedence over costs to continue the off-shore operations. The trend of shifting to alternative lower economies has also been observed. Particularly for global operations, one should also consider the transaction issues in relation to the fluctuation of currency exchange and different payment/transaction practices.

Quality. When offshore operations take place, activities such as sourcing and production are harder to control. All these would be subject to the reliability of suppliers, and, therefore, it is beyond the full control of an organization. As a result, the quality of products and services becomes more difficult to be guaranteed. This is also due to the lack of visibility of upstream supply chain partners' operations and practices. As a global supply chain involves longer logistics connections, ensuring the quality and precision of transportation, which affect the products and services, is also a big challenge. Thus, the relationship with supply chain partners is paramount in reducing the risks of the substandard quality of products and services.

Speed. To control the speed in terms of bringing the products to the market is one obvious challenge in the global supply chain context as the chain has been extended to an international scale and more players are involved. Production delays, delivery disruption, and lack of communication are the factors to be addressed to avoid any unnecessary interruption leading to a longer lead time.

Dependability. This challenge is predominantly related to the performance of supply chain partners in the network, which is one key factor in efficient global supply chain management. It is critical to select the right partners who are reliable in keeping their promises in terms of agreed schedules, delivery, prices, and other commitments.

Flexibility. It is a challenge to maintain the operational flexibility of a global supply chain if it is managed onshore. This includes the flexibility of provisions of product mix and volume, introducing new products to the market and alternative resources/materials used. This could be translated as the agility of facilities and practices in place to cope with changes and variation of demands in the global operations. The agility of delivery arrangement is also a key to complement the above-mentioned flexibility.

As discussed earlier, we see how globalization has made the supply chain management more complex and segregated from different aspects. Operations managers must carefully analyze the global market environment, assess the trade-off of decisions and practices, and develop the right strategy and plan. Despite new challenges faced by businesses, this lends itself to opportunities to manage global supply chain operations more efficiently and advantages of globalization. The key issue is how operations managers can capitalize these opportunities.

These opportunities could be examined from a few dimensions. Since the market has become global, Bowersox et al. (2012), Jonsson (2008), and Grant et al. (2006) identified the opportunity of forming business alliances and developing new partnership or joint ventures to benefit the offshore business. This is an ideal strategy to access new market with shared ownership and operate on counter-trade, and, hence, risks sharing/minimizing. This extends to the possibility of licensing or franchising for some businesses, and stimulating more importing and exporting activities to take advantage of the lower sourcing and larger market coverage, respectively. Its potential also includes addressing the five challenges discussed earlier, that is, reducing cost, increasing speed and flexibility, and improving quality and dependability, through sharing information and resources (such as manufacturing facilities, transportation, labor, materials, and other assets).

As discussed in the previous section, the visibility of operations at a global scale is an issue; therefore, investing in technology and the information system would be essential to increase the visibility to ensure that any ramification could be put in place in case of any supply chain disruption. For example, RFID has been a popular automatic track and trace tool in the market to provide real-time information and status of tagged items in the supply chain. Any irregularity when transporting items from one stage to another in the supply chain will be made aware almost instantly. As the global market is subject to a higher degree of uncertainty and variation of demands and expectations, information technology (IT) such as EDI, vendor/supplier-managed inventory (VMI/SMI), WMS, customer-managed order, quick response (QR), efficient consumer response (ECR), and collaborative planning forecasting and replenishment (CPFR), could be implemented and integrated to better manage the extended operations and strengthen the partnership with offshore suppliers or customers. More on technology innovation will be discussed in the following section.

In logistics operations, there are opportunities to address the five challenges by means of re-assessing existing inventory planning, warehousing operations, and storage requirements, as well as transportation arrangement for global operations. For instance, with new international partnership formed, certain stacking of goods in the warehouse can be avoided through transhipment within the partners' network, and storage requirement can also be reduced through sharing warehouse facilities. Therefore, the warehouse spaces to own can be scaled down accordingly. Similarly, this also applies to transportation arrangement.

To cope with different markets, operations managers could encourage their organizations to practice generic or modular product design for multiple markets to avoid product proliferation depending on the nature of the product. For instance, multiple languages are pre-installed in a mobile device for a number of markets rather than different languages for different markets. In this regard, Bowersox et al. (2012) also suggested other global operational considerations, such as performance features, technical characteristics, environmental issues, and health and safety requirements. Careful planning to address these operational issues will provide an opportunity to drive down overall product unit cost and lead time, and increase the ability to respond quickly to demands around the globe.

4.4 THE ROLE OF INNOVATION IN ACHIEVING EFFICIENT GLOBAL SUPPLY CHAIN OPERATIONS

As we have discussed the impacts, challenges, and opportunities resulting from global supply chain operations in previous sections, this section aims to inspire operations managers through examining the role of innovation to enhance achieving the efficient and cost-effective global operations.

As presented in Chapter 1, Section 1.4, innovation can be related to the design of new products and services to offer, as well as redesign existing operations and practices in a novel way. Either innovation can lead to radical (breakthrough) or incremental (continuous) change of products and services. Great examples have been provided in the same chapter. In Chapter 1, we have discussed about the type of innovation, namely, organizational, managerial, operational, process, service, product, and commercial/marketing innovation. These different types of innovations will not take place in isolation. Initiating innovation in one dimension will have an impact on the other. For instance, introducing new product innovation, for example, manufacturing products in the modular form will relate to how the product is manufactured and designed—operational and process innovation. Therefore, quite often we see that organizations set up a cross-functional team consisting of members of staff from different departments across the organization to jointly initiate innovation for business improvement to ensure that all aspects of business functions are considered. The stages involved have also been discussed in Chapter 1, Section 1.6.

This section aims to build on what has been discussed in Chapter 2, exploring innovation in improving operations, which will directly impact customers, and hence are critical in ensuring efficient global supply chain management. Innovation, in this context, refers to doing something different in a creative way, aiming to achieve better performance in any possible dimension. Regardless of whether it is radical or incremental innovation, it involves novelty, change, invention, creativity, and better design.

Although some decisions may have to be made by the senior management team, they will be cascaded down onto the operational level that requires different operational innovation to take place. Therefore, concurrent innovation planning and design should take place simultaneously across different functions to ensure effective execution plans will be produced, which is similar to the approach of concurrent engineering in operations management practice. Considering the five challenges above, design and sourcing teams will ensure the product's quality, logistics department will ensure on time delivery (speed), production team will ensure dependability and flexibility capabilities, and ultimately, all these teams work together to lower the overall cost incurred.

We will assess the potential of innovation to achieve efficient global supply chain operations in two aspects: the technology innovation and innovative operations improvement.

Technology innovation. In recent years, we have seen that more and more business operations are technology-driven and dependent, and the role of technology has become central to many improvement programs. Hence, the innovative use of technology is crucial to bring the existing operations to another level of improvement and to be more sustainable. RFID has been identified as one of the greatest influencing technologies for the modern twenty-first century digital, knowledge-based economy (Lim, et al. 2013). It is an automatic identification and data capture (AIDC) technology using radio waves to transmit data between the transponders (i.e., tags) and transceivers (readers), and have attracted significant attention in the fields of supply chain and manufacturing, as well as various service sectors (Hunt, et al. 2007). Businesses have benefited from RFID implementation through improvements in operations efficiency and cost savings, and opportunities for generating greater revenues. The typical benefits of using RFID over barcoding include the unique identification of tagged items, improved stock visibility, traceability and status monitoring at each stage in supply chains, increased data accuracy and sharing, eliminated manual inventory counts, automated receiving and scanning, and so on.

Operations managers need to explore innovative gains in various supply chain operations beyond the existing proven benefits; Lim et al. (2013) have discussed the RFID's potential in logistics/warehouse operations, alongside its future development integrating with other advanced technology. Other emerging technologies, such as Internet of Things (IoT) and Cloud Computing (Internet), have great potential for integration with RFID in global supply chain operations. IoT connects various sensors of entities, and with RFID-tagging, these sensing data can be collected in real time and shared through Cloud Computing with global business partners. By innovatively leveraging and integrating these technologies and combining their unique characteristics, a company can explore global supply chain management. Furthermore, incorporating other *soft* systems, such as artificial intelligence (AI) and expert systems, would further enhance its potential. For instance, once some disruptions (say breakdown of facilities) were detected in the supply chain through RFID/IoT, then AI could be used with collected real-time data and historical data/solutions to intelligently identify key actions through the instant evaluation of current conditions and reconfiguration/optimization of the supply chain network. The five challenges could be quickly addressed to ensure that the best solution is implemented. Big data analysis will also further create values from the collected data.

In terms of business IT, we have seen various software systems in use in supply chain operations, for instance, enterprise resource planning (ERP), WMS, materials requirement planning (MRP), customer relationship management (CRM), EDI and web-EDI, transport management system (TMS), advance planning and scheduling (APS), and so on. The use of these IT systems has improved different supply chain operations. However, being innovative in integrating these IT systems with, for example, RFID for real-time data collection and IoT/Cloud Computing for the instant ramification of resolving issues could further enhance the potential of greater reap of benefits.

In this modern and advanced world, we are embraced with all types of technologies in our daily life. Smart phones/mobile tablets are now becoming essential for most people; thus, there is great potential for companies to leverage the use of global positioning system (GPS), mobile apps, and near-field communication (NFC) functions available in the phones. Devices with these technologies record delivery and real-time update for business partners and are, therefore, useful for customers. Once integrated with CRM, it will strengthen the relationship with the customers, and when that with the WMS, it will ensure that inventory stock-out does not occur.

Innovative operations improvement. There is a wide range of approaches, tools, and techniques available for operations improvement, each with its specific purpose of use for a certain aspect or method of improvement. It is very often that a set of improvement tools and techniques are selected to improve a specific operation. Each business improvement expert may have a different piece of advice; which one to use depends on what to achieve. When we try to improve our operations, we need to first identify the causes of the problems. Tools that can commonly be used to identify these include cause and effect diagrams, statistical process control, Pareto analysis, flowcharts, control charts, run charts, check sheets, bar charts, scatter diagrams, matrix analysis, tally chart, and histograms (Dale et al. 2007). Some of these tools are also useful when we need to measure the quality performance based on the data collected. To examine the relationship between processes, we could employ the process mapping and value stream mapping approaches. These can also identify problems and non-value-added activities. These methods are discussed in more detail in Chapter 10.

The Lean principle is a popular improvement approach that aims to reduce all wastes possible and use as minimal resources as possible. The popular Lean tools and techniques are 5s, Six Sigma, JIT (Just in Time), Kaizen (continuous improvement), Kanban (pull system), MUDA (waste reduction), overall equipment effectiveness, plan–do–check–act (PDCA) model, Poka-Yoke method, root cause analysis, single-minute exchange of dies (SMED), Takt time, total productive maintenance, and so on. Total quality management (TQM) is a management approach to improve operations from the quality's perspective. There are eight key elements of TQM, namely, ethics, integrity, trust, training, teamwork, leadership, recognition, and communication. Other methods include quality function deployment (QFD), failure mode and effects analysis (FMEA), business process reengineering (BPR), and hypothesis testing and simulation. When practicing the technology innovation, it will also relate to operations improvement, which will put the above-mentioned tools and techniques in good use.

Putting the five challenges' and globalization's hat on, we can re-assess, with any existing tools and techniques available, the current operations and think outside the box to identify an innovative way to create new improvement opportunities. Especially in global operations, one can jointly re-assess and re-implement the tools with their global partners in order to achieve truly global supply chain efficiency. Jonsson (2008) suggested redesigning supply chains to consider vertically versus laterally integrated supply chains and responsive (agile) versus physically efficient (Lean) supply chains.

To be innovative in improving operations in a globalization context, we should be creative in exploring, leveraging, and maximizing the potentials of the tools, techniques, approaches, as well as technologies to benefit the entire global supply chain operations. For instance, when we plan our global operations to be Leaner, we first need to have a great visibility of each activity in the extended supply chain. We could implement RFID and IoT technologies, with online real-time track and trace capability, to capture the lead time of each activity and measure all dimensions of performance instantly, and with the data collected, we could then use the above-mentioned improvement tools and techniques to identify the value-added and non-value-added activities. With these data made available, we could have an intelligence tool in place to dynamically optimize the entire operations and generate the best solution for global operations improvement.

4.5 SUMMARY

As globalization is taking place, businesses are facing greater and greater challenges in ensuring efficiency in managing the extended supply chains. When we analyze these challenges thoroughly, it also gives us a great opportunity to achieve competitive advantage through innovative thinking, leading to creative integrated approaches that could be applied across the multitier supply chain system along with global partners. This could ensure ultimate reap of benefits resulting from globalization practices.

This chapter set the scene by discussing the impact of globalization to supply chains, naming a few such as longer lead time, higher risk of disruption, limited visibility of operations, quality as well as supplier issues. The discussion on today's challenges resulting from globalization is based on the operational measurements of performance proposed by Slack et al. (2016), which are cost, quality, speed, flexibility, and dependability. Deriving from challenges, opportunities can be identified from a more strategic level to an operational level. Furthermore, this chapter demonstrated the role of innovation in enhancing the potential benefits resulting from globalization practices, which can be scrutinized from the technology's and operations improvement's perspectives.

KEY POINTS TO REMEMBER

- Globalization is now a norm in doing business.
- Existing supply chain practices may be obsolete or have potential for significant improvement and therefore need to be re-assessed.
- We first need to understand the impact of globalization to supply chains.
- We then identify the challenges faced; each industry/sector will have different challenges resulting from globalization practices.
- Five operational measurements of performance, namely, cost, quality, speed, flexibility, and dependability, could be used to transform the challenges into opportunities to take advantage of globalization.
- The role of innovation is crucial to realize these opportunities, leading to impactful solutions for business improvement and growth.
- Innovative thinking should be applied to creatively leverage the modern technologies, integrating with improvement tools or techniques in the new horizon of the supply chain system.
- Modern technologies include RFID, IoT, Cloud Computing, NFC, GPS, and a range of IT systems for different supply chain operations.
- Improvement approaches, tools, and techniques include the Lean principle (e.g., Kanban, Six Sigma, Kaizen, etc.), TQM, QFD, and others.

CASE STUDY

Emirates Airline Operations—Globalization Effect

Balan Sundarakani

Associate Professor and Programme Director, MSc Logistics
University of Wollongong in Dubai, UAE

INTRODUCTION

By December 2016, demand for the top seven airline players had grown by an average of 4.5% year-over-year (IATA, 2017), and Emirates had remained as one of the top carriers in the world. However, the financial impact of weak oil prices had been the cause of slower growth in the Middle East, as it led to lower levels of economic activity in the region. According to new forecasts issued by the ratings agency Moody, in 2017 the Middle East is set to be the fastest growing region of the world for the airline industry (Forbes, 2017). Good supply chain management practices and a properly designed supply chain strategy play a crucial role in the success of today's airline supply chain landscape. But a world-renowned airline such as Emirates Airline (EA) in its 28 years of service despite having faced global uncertainties had still kept the airline highly profitable.

EMIRATES AIRLINE BACKGROUND

EA was formed in 1985 with the support of Dubai's royal family and with only US$10 million in start-up capital. The first two aircrafts were wet leased from Pakistan International Airline. On October 25, 1985 the first flight of Emirates EK600 departed from the Dubai International Airport to Karachi. Karachi, New Delhi, and Mumbai were the first three destinations of EA. In 1986 the network grew into Amman, Colombo, Cairo, and Dhaka. Further investment was later made in infrastructure and further expansion costs saw Emirates posting losses in 1986 for the first and actually last time. From that point forward, Emirates saw profits soaring year after year, with

(Continued)

more and more destinations being added to its network and increasing passenger miles and fleet size. Currently, Emirates flies to 128 destinations with a fleet size of 199 aircrafts (Emirates, 2017).

The goal of EA has always been quality and not quantity. It strives to provide the highest level of service to its customers. This is the secret of Emirates' success. Over the year, EA has grown in scale and stature not through protectionism but through competition. Emirates follows and encourages the open-skies policy. Continuing its explosive growth, the airline has diversified its business into different streams like international cargo division, full-fledged destination management, leisure division, and an airline IT developer.

Emirates with its continuous growth has now its own dedicated terminal, that is, Terminal-3 for its operations. Currently it is the world's largest operator of Airbus A380 and Boeing B777. EA's current order stands at more than 230 aircrafts, which sums up to about US$84 billion. Emirates has one of the youngest and most modern fleet in the commercial aviation industry. The overall goal of Emirates is to keep providing world-class service to its customers and to develop Dubai into a complete, worldwide, long-haul aviation hub (Emirates, 2017).

EMIRATES AIRLINE SUPPLY CHAIN STRATEGY

In today's world, supply chain strategies (SCE) form a very essential spine of businesses. Being able to cover key markets effectively by making sure that products are available to these depends on the effectiveness of an SCE. Globalization creates an avenue for market reach, but at the same time it poses challenges. Therefore, having an effective SCE is essential for the success of EA's operations. In order to deliver the best SCE, it is essential to have the right competitive strategy. An organization should first work on building a sustainable competitive strategy that is right for its service/product segment. Once the competitive strategy is set, then an organization should work on building its supply chain strategy.

EA's competitive strategy is to provide a world-class service to their customers. Its aim is to provide quality to its customers and not quantity, and Emirates tries to do so at the lowest possible cost.

(Continued)

TABLE CS4.1

Supply Chain Strategy of Emirates Airline

Driver	Emirates Airline—Supply Chain Strategy
Facility	Responsive (with little efficiency)
Inventory	Highly responsive supply chain
Transportation	Hybrid supply chain strategy
Information	Hybrid supply chain strategy
Sourcing	Hybrid supply chain strategy
Pricing	Hybrid (more toward responsiveness)
Overall	Hybrid (more toward responsiveness)

Based on this competitive strategy, Emirates built on its SCE. Its supply chain strategy is a hybrid of being efficient and responsive, but it is more inclined toward responsiveness. Emirates supply chain success is also related to the right mixture and integration of logistic and cross-functional drivers as shown in Table CS4.1.

EMIRATES AIRLINE OPERATIONAL STRATEGY

EA being such a large organization has many operations within its supply chain, where the end result is to provide a high-quality service and level of customer satisfaction by transporting customers from one place to another on time. Thus, in order to achieve this competitive strategy, Emirates has tried to optimize its operational strategies to the maximum.

Firstly, Emirates maintains the youngest fleet in the world, with a life span of 8 to 12 years, hence minimizing the maintenance and repair costs drastically. Second, the most important element that Emirates has come up with is the use of an ultramain system. This system has made the management of materials, procurement of materials, warranty management, and maintenance-related activities of data management easy. This one software has concentrated the work of entire engineering into one location, making the management of data much more efficient, accurate, and readily available to everyone. Figure CS4.1 shows one of the two modules in which this software is divided.

(Continued)

FIGURE CS4.1
Module 1 of ultramain system (Emirates Engineering Training).

The operational strategy of EA has also been putting more and more effort on the online sales or sales through its Airline Call Centre. Emirates has achieved this by building an international site that is available in more than 30 languages. It has also set up one of the world's best call centres in Dubai. This operational strategy has helped Emirates in saving huge costs such as commission costs, incentives, and so on that are paid to the travel agents.

Another operational strategy of EA is the point-to-point transit. Point-to-point transit helps in saving huge costs by eliminating the need for ground equipment and maintenance personnel in each location where the aircraft transits through. In this case, there is only one main hub for EA, that is, Dubai Airport, and all flights fly to and from this hub to their final destinations. This requires the concentration of equipment, maintenance personnel, and other support services to be made available only in the central hub or the final destination, hence eliminating all unnecessary costs of landing, parking, and so on present in transit hubs. Also, it reduces travel time and removes the hassle of connecting flights, hence eliminating the domino effect.

Long haul flights are another operational strategy of EA. This long haul flight model has drastically increased the profits for Emirates compared to the expensive short haul flights (The Economist, 2013). The operating costs have been reduced by 15%–20%, hence increasing the profit. This benefit has also been passed onto the customers, who are getting tickets for the same routes at almost 30% lower price compared to competitors, but Emirates providing higher quality and customer satisfaction.

Another operational strategy of emirates is its flexible workforce. A blend of Emirates Lean labor force and young fleet accounts for

(Continued)

its outstanding low cost and a tough cost-based competitive profile. The labor-activated low cost is formed by a very Lean labor force, equivalent to leading low-cost carriers rather than other conventional carriers. This, along with a simpler flat organizational structure, allows the airline to lower overhead costs. Also, employees' turnover is low due to its extensive investment in training and keeping employees up to date, reducing their operational costs in return.

Delays are a major concern for any airline as they can be costly. For EA this is a serious issue and hence they have put forward stringent measures to ensure on-time departures and arrivals. They measure this through on-time performance (OTP). Emirates has a policy where passengers need to be at the check-in counter no later than 90 minutes before departure and should be at the boarding gate no later than 45 minutes from the departure time. One of the measures EA has put in place is to make sure that each staff carries out his or her role in a well-coordinated manner so that the domino effect of failures/problems is minimized. Domino effect is that in which a delay in a flight from a location will result in a delay in its following arrivals and departures, and the chain will continue. But in such case, pilots, ground personnel, and engineers should be ready in advance to face this issue by trying their best to minimize the delay by taking the desired measures as a group. This in turn saves major delay costs for Emirates and keeps customers happy by transporting them on time to their destinations.

Branding and marketing constitute an important aspect of the success of any operational strategy. EA has a dynamic branding approach. It keeps coming up with innovative ideas to brand and promote itself. It invests in sponsorship of events and international sports, the most recent being the Formula 1. EA keeps updating its slogan to match up with the ever-evolving world and mesmerize its current and potential customers. For instance, it recently changed its slogan from *Keep Discovering* to *Hello Tomorrow*.

Expanding its network across the world is another strategy that EA is currently practicing, that is, the strategy of global expansion. In 2012, Emirates expanded to as much as 15 routes and is still

(Continued)

expanding to more routes, being one of the highest in airline industry. Currently, 128 destinations are being served by Emirates.

Having discussed that, EA has applied the operational strategy of providing innovative and exceptional services/products to its customers. This has increased its customer numbers, which in return has contributed to an increase in its profit and market share. As seen earlier, these are some of the operational strategies practiced by Emirates Airline to achieve its competitive strategy of providing quality and high level of customer service to their customers at reasonable costs.

ACKNOWLEDGMENT

The author would like to acknowledge the support provided by Abhishek Sood, Guruprakash Kaliyaperumal, and Mohammad Ali Javed in collecting the secondary data used as the basis for the case study and providing support to enhancing its quality.

REFERENCES

The Economist. (2013). Up and Away. Available: http://www.economist.com/blogs/schumpeter/2013/11/dubai-air-show?zid=308&ah=e21d923f9b263c5548d5615da3d30f4d (Accessed December 6, 2013).

Forbes. (2017). Middle East To Lead Global Airline Industry Growth This Year. Available: http://www.forbes.com/sites/dominicdudley/2017/01/17/middle-east-airline-industry-growth/#44cae1b82498 (Accessed February 1, 2017).

IATA. (2017). International Air Travel Association, 2017. Available: http://www.iata.org/about/Pages/mission.aspx (Accessed January 28, 2017).

Emirates. (2017). The Emirates Group—Emirates Airline Overview. Available: http://www.theemiratesgroup.com/english/images/04_EK_Overview_tcm409-560539.pdf (Accessed January 28, 2017).

REFERENCES

Bowersox, D.J., Closs, D.J., and Cooper, M.B. (2012). *Supply Chain Logistics Management*. New York, NY: McGraw-Hill.

Burt, D.N., Petcavage, S.D., and Pinkerton, R.L. (2010). *Supply Management*. New York, NY: McGraw-Hill.

Dale, B.G., van der Wiele, T., and van Iwaarden, J. (2007). *Managing Quality*. Malden, MA: Wiley-Blackwell.

Grant, D.B., Lambert, D., Stock, J.R., and Ellram, L.M. (2006). *Fundamentals of Logistics Management*. Maindenhead, UK: McGraw-Hill Higher Education.

Hunt, V.D., Puglia, M., Puglia, A. (2007). *A Guide to Radio Frequency Identification.* Hoboken, NJ: John Wiley & Sons.

Jonsson, P. (2008). *Logistics and Supply Chain Management.* Maidenhead, UK: McGraw-Hill Higher Education.

Lim, M., Bahr, W., and Leung, S.C.H. (2013). RFID in the Warehouse: A Literature Analysis (1995–2010) of its applications, benefits, challenges and future trends. *International Journal of Production Economics* 145(1): 409–430.

Lipsey, R. (2001). PwC's opacity index: A powerful new tool for global investors. *Journal of Corporate Accounting & Finance* 12(6): 35–44.

Murphy, P.R. and Knemeyer, A.M. (2015). *Contemporary Logistics.* Essex, UK: Pearson Education.

Neely, A. (Ed.) (2011). *Business Performance Measurement.* Cambridge, MA: Cambridge University Press.

Ritson, N. (2008). *Strategic Management.* New York, NY: Neil Rotson & Ventus Publishing.

Simchi-Levi, D., Kaminsky, P., and Simchi-Levi, E. (2009). *Designing and Managing the Supply Chain: Concepts, Strategies, and Case Studies.* New York, NY: McGraw-Hill.

Slack, N., Chambers, S., and Johnston, R. (2016). *Operations Management,* 8th ed. Harlow, UK: Pearson.

FURTHER SUGGESTED READING

Rushton, A., Croucher, P., and Baker, P. (2014). *The Handbook of Logistics and Distribution Management,* 5th ed. London, UK: Kogan Page.

Section III

Understanding
the Internal Context

Section III

Understanding
the Internal Context

5

The Role of Operations Managers in Building a Culture of Innovation and Continuous Improvement

5.1 INTRODUCTION

It is often common to find in industry that the focus of managers in many innovation and improvement efforts lies on using well-known approaches and making sure that the staff involved in these projects have the right skills to use the appropriate tools. However, an essential part when implementing innovation or improvement initiatives is paying attention to the *soft skills*. To succeed in these and other change initiatives, employees must be fully committed as well as engaged being part of the process. For this reason, and after having dedicated the initial four chapters to discuss general and *external* aspects that affect the innovation and operations of organizations, in this chapter, we focus on discussing some key aspects that operations managers must consider to create a culture of innovation and continuous improvement within their organizations. In particular, this chapter provides some insights into the relationship that exists between organizational culture and innovation and continuous improvement. Then, it defines and provides some insights into how the organizational characteristics that facilitate innovation may be developed. Finally, we also offer some suggestions regarding how employees can be engaged in innovation and continuous improvement efforts.

5.2 ORGANIZATIONAL CULTURE AND ITS RELATION TO INNOVATION AND CONTINUOUS IMPROVEMENT

Organizational culture plays a significant role in innovation creation and continuous improvement. This culture is normally deeply embedded in organization's core values and employees' behavior and personalities. According to Reigle (2001), culture of an organization is a reflection of their commitment to succeed in innovation activities. Organizational culture can, therefore, positively influence and motivate employees, resulting in the easy acceptance and commitment toward innovation-related customs embedded within their organizations. This signifies that organizations embarking on the continuous improvement- and innovation-led journey based on a process-based approach (see Chapter 1) should foster the right thinking, behavior, and beliefs among their employees. However, the key question is: What type of thinking, behavior, and beliefs operations managers must foster within their employees to successfully enhance processes through either continuous improvement or operational innovation? The section attempts to answer this question. However, before we answer this question, let us first try to identify the most common types of organizational cultures that exist, and relate them to the innovation and continuous improvement cultures.

Over the years, various researchers have proposed a number of ways to classify organizational culture; however, the classification proposed by Handy (1993) is most widely accepted. Handy (1993) classifies organizational culture into four main types, namely, role culture, power culture, person culture, and task culture. Among these, the first two are most commonly evident in industries that are discussed in the following. It is very important for managers to understand the culture of their own organizations as it can assist them in knowing how far their organization is from the desired cultural state that nurtures innovation and continuous improvement.

- The most common culture that normally exists in an organization is the *role culture*. In this form of culture, the tasks within the organizations are logical and rationally divided such as the use of functional departments (e.g., operations, purchasing, finance, human resources, and so on). Organizations following the role culture are guided and coordinated by managers who exert control through strict rules and regulations. Hence, this form of bureaucratic culture is mostly evident in large and well-established organizations. The evidence reported in upcoming chapters will show that the role culture is normally not supportive of innovation since the procedures and rules often act as barriers for employees in proposing innovative ideas to carry out the organization's operations. However, it will be difficult to imagine organizations that do not follow any procedures and rules, as some sorts of control are always required to operate efficiently. Therefore, it is challenging for operations managers engaged in building the culture of innovation in an organization following a role culture to foster creative thinking (i.e., innovation) without losing the control of the operations and hence efficiency. A classic example as to how efficiency and innovation can be balanced is that of Google, which gives its employees 20% of their work time to pursue projects that they feel passionate about, regardless of whether those project ideas are outside of their core job responsibilities or the core mission of the organization. Most of these creative project ideas are focused on finding better ways of doing things. The role culture does favor more a kaizen (i.e., continuous improvement) cultural approach, thus focusing on small, gradual, and consistent improvement steps without requiring any radical changes within the organization. Therefore, changes tend not to deviate greatly from the ways of doing things guided by the rules and regulations.

- The second most commonly found culture within organizations is the *power culture*. This form of culture depends on a central source of power that influences the entire organization. This type of culture is commonly evident in small organizations. Compared to organizations that follow the role culture, organizations following the power culture tend to have less rules and regulations; however, there is no evidence to suggest that these are more innovative. Similar to the challenges faced by operations managers in role culture, here also managers must find a balanced approach promoting innovation without losing those controls to ensure that the organization operates efficiently.

5.2.1 Characteristic of Innovative Cultures

The previous section discussed the two most widely used organizational cultures and their relations to the innovation and continuous improvement culture. It is, therefore, now important to identify characteristics supportive of both cultures that operations managers need to foster within their employees and organizations. In this direction, Von Stamm (2008) identifies experimentation, collaboration and competition, fun and focus, and commitment to innovation as four main characteristics that promote innovation culture. Operations managers can focus on developing these characteristics to achieve operational innovation.

- Experimentation has emerged as one of the key cultural characteristics that operations managers should foster to be innovative. Operations managers believing in experimentation constantly challenge the status quo of the current operations to seek opportunities to improve them and motivate their employees to do the same. The innovation process reviewed in Chapter 1 (Section 1.6) can be used to identify potential ways to improve operations and later experiments with them once the status quo has been challenged. For experimentation to be successful, operations managers must also develop three other *subcultural characteristics*: acceptance of failure, project termination, and *can do* attitude. It is a common understanding that not all the plausible ways to improve operations may always be effective or adequate for each scenario. Hence, operations managers need to foster a culture where failure is accepted and used as an opportunity of learning from experience. They should be quick in identifying unsuccessful potential ways and abandoning them as soon as possible. In addition, they should encourage a *can do* culture, that is, employees should be free to try things out and experiment without a need to request permission in most cases. However, this is only feasible when the organization is willing to accept failures as a likely outcome of experimentation with different and novel ways to achieve operational improvements.
- Collaboration at both internal and external levels is a normal trait of organizations following innovation culture. Hence, operations managers intending to improve operations must focus on developing a culture that encourages close collaboration with core and support functions within the organizations as well as customers, suppliers, and, in general, all key stakeholders. A simple example to support this notion is of Unipart Group, a multinational

logistics, supply chain, manufacturing, and consultancy organization headquartered in Cowley, Oxfordshire, UK, that encourages cross-departmental collaboration and includes representatives of customers, suppliers, and transportation groups in its operation improvement activities. Apart from collaboration, some innovative organizations also believe in the value of internal and external competition. Hence, operations managers should also create a competitive environment among their employees such as rewarding the employee who proposes the best approach to operational improvement. Many successful organizations such as American Express and AT&T often sponsor online creativity contests to inspire innovation among their customers.

- The third important innovative culture characteristic is fun, exploration, and play, which Von Stamm (2008) identifies as a fruitful ground for operations managers, particularly in the manufacturing industry where operation procedures are rigid and well established, and are expected to be followed. This is often a challenge for operations managers; however, if they are able to cultivate a fun-filled and explorative atmosphere without losing focus, and ideas and suggestions are encouraged, *failure* will be more bearable.

- Innovative organizations are fully committed to innovation even when they are going through difficult economic times as they continue to invest in innovative teams and projects, and implement supportive policies. Thus, ideally, improvements through operational innovation must be part of the day-to-day operations of an organization independent of the organization's current economic status. However, in most cases during hardships, innovation and improvement projects are among the first activities canceled. Therefore, it is the task of operations managers to convince the top management of the value of innovative projects and highlighting the medium- to long-term benefits of those activities for the organization.

5.2.2 Characteristic of Continuous Improvement Cultures

So far we have discussed about innovation culture; however, there is also another type of culture, that is, that of continuous improvement known as kaizen culture in Lean manufacturing terminology. This form of culture enables an organization and its employees to adapt a set of philosophies, principles, and tools toward improving operations, products, and services. In the operational context, the primary difference between innovation and continuous improvement culture is that the focus of the former is to find new (i.e., radical) inventive and better ways to operate and improve processes, whereas the latter strives for an endless pursuit of improvement. However, organizations must develop certain *adaptive* characteristics before they can adopt the continuous improvement culture and become better at improving and teaching others how to improve (Miller et al. 2014). Therefore, operations managers' effort must be to ensure that their teams and organizations first possess, or develop, the following adaptive characteristics, which will serve as preliminary facilitators to achieve a continuous improvement culture.

- Customer-focused
- Proactive
- Taking intelligent risks
- Information flows quickly and smoothly
- Local decision-making and initiative encouraged
- High creativity

Readers interested to gain a deeper insight into particular aspects of creating a continuous improvement culture can explore the work of Miller et al. (2014), Hope et al. (2011), and Haeckel (1999).

Once the adaptive characteristics have been developed, operations managers should ensure that following (see bullet points) cultural elements are reflected as parts of the attitudes and behaviors of their employees and organization's work culture. These elements, although not an all-inclusive list, provide guidance to operations managers as to what some common characteristics of this culture are so that they know what attitudes and behaviors they must seek, encourage, and sustain within their teams and organizations.

- Broad participation and engagement of all staff, who relentlessly search for opportunities to improve and work together
- Management by processes

- Team-based factual problem solving
- Visual management and measurements
- The workplace is clean, orderly, and safe
- Visionary leadership

Readers can refer to the work of Jekiel (2011) and Van Aartsengel and Kurtoglu (2013) for a deeper understanding of how to develop such elements. In many cases, continuous improvement is associated with particular management practices aimed at identifying and realizing opportunities for better performance; however, one should also realize that this form of culture goes beyond these management practices.

5.2.3 An Innovation or a Continuous Improvement Culture?

The discussion presented earlier in this chapter may lead to the question: Which culture operations managers should adopt for their organizations? We suggest that operations managers should not make a choice between the two; rather, they should foment the characteristics of both as they complement each other. There is already evidence of such practices in organizations. For example, Toyota is well known for aggressively pursuing continuous improvement programs in their operations based on the Deming's PDCA (i.e., plan–do–check–act) improvement cycle which is already well embedded in kaizen (i.e., continuous improvement) culture. However, Toyota is also aware of the fact that in some cases, it is essential to complement and combine the incremental improvements with operational innovations that can provide quick radical improvement and which can involve even complete redesign of certain aspects of its well established processes. This is not surprising as Grover and Kettinger (1998) discusses that this is a common case in industry, where many organizations often combine radical (i.e., operational innovation) and incremental (i.e., continuous improvement) initiatives. Often organizations may innovate by radically designing new operations however then implement short-term incremental improvements on this operation. This shows that both approaches to improvement are perfectly compatible and therefore to obtain better results, they should be combined. Hence, operations managers should aim at developing cultural characteristics and elements supportive of the effective adoption of both approaches.

5.3 RECOGNIZING AND DEVELOPING THE ORGANIZATIONAL CHARACTERISTICS THAT FACILITATE INNOVATION

In the earlier sections, we identified and discussed the various characteristics and elements that operations managers must develop to build a culture of innovation and continuous improvement. However, it is likely that there would be some other factors, besides culture, which will play an important role in the creation of an innovative organization. A number of factors have been identified by researchers. For example, Van der Panne et al. (2003) identified four factors: firm-related, project-related, product-related, and market-related. In this chapter, however, we focus on only the firm-related factor that operation managers can stimulate to improve the innovation capability of an organization, and those interested in a full review of all other factors can refer to the work of Trott (2017). These factors present an opportunity for operations managers to improve innovation performance; hence, they need to develop these factors in their organizations. In conjunction with the attitudes and behaviors (i.e., cultural characteristics), the organizational characteristics identified in what follows will also contribute to the facilitation and success of the innovation process reviewed in Chapter 1, Section 1.6. Table 5.1 presents a full list of firm-related factors, as identified by Trott (2017), and a brief correlation with those that can be stimulated by operations managers either within their own team, in an organizational function, or in the entire organization.

To summarize the discussion so far, operations managers willing to put their organizations on the innovation pathway and implement operational innovation must aim to put in place and develop the factors marked as *yes* in Table 5.1 within their teams, functional supportive areas, and the entire organization.

TABLE 5.1

Role of Operations Managers and Its Relation to the Organizational Characteristics that Facilitate Innovation

Organizational Requirement (Factor) for Innovation	Can It Be Overseen (Affected) by an Operations Manager?		Comment
	Yes	No	
1. Growth orientation *It refers to the commitment of an organization to long-term growth instead of short-term profits*		✓	The corporate strategy will mainly dictate this factor, and the operations function may only provide some input for the formulation of such a strategy. However, the operations function will most probably not affect the growth orientation of a company directly and to a great extent
2. Organizational heritage and innovation experience *This factor is characterized by a widespread recognition of the values of innovation*	✓ (Limited influence)		This will come from the culture and history of an organization. Operations managers may be able to convince the employees and the organization, in general, about the value of innovation while at the same time influencing some cultural innovation aspects
3. Vigilance and external links *It refers to the ability of an organization to be aware of its opportunities and treats*	✓ (Limited influence)		This will be part of the mechanisms put in place by the organization to *scan* its external competitive environment. Operations managers may raise the awareness of the need for this type of mechanism and to contribute in their design. They will also be able to recognize external operational treats and opportunities, and make aware the company of these

(Continued)

TABLE 5.1 (Continued)

Role of Operations Managers and Its Relation to the Organizational Characteristics that Facilitate Innovation

Organizational Requirement (Factor) for Innovation	Can It Be Overseen (Affected) by an Operations Manager?		Comment
	Yes	No	
4. Commitment to technology and R&D intensity *This factor is related to the willingness of a company to invest in the development of technology in the long term*		✓	The operations function will have very little, or no input, on this factor as it will be mainly dictated by the corporate strategy of the company
5. Acceptance of risks *This is characterized by the willingness to include risky opportunities in a balanced portfolio*	✓		Operations managers may be able to influence certain aspects of this culture-related factor; see Section 5.2
6. Cross-functional cooperation and coordination within the organizational structure *This factor refers to the mutual willingness to work together across functions and mutual respect among individuals*	✓		Operations managers may greatly influence this factor at any of the three levels, namely entire organization, function, or team levels; see Section 5.2
7. Receptivity *The ability to be aware of, identify, and take advantage of externally developed technology*	✓		Operations managers may be able to promote this company's wide characteristic throughout the organization or within their own functions. Also, in some cases, they will be able to adapt externally developed technologies for the benefit of their own company's operations and processes

(Continued)

TABLE 5.1 (Continued)

Role of Operations Managers and Its Relation to the Organizational Characteristics that Facilitate Innovation

Organizational Requirement (Factor) for Innovation	Can It Be Overseen (Affected) by an Operations Manager?		Comment
	Yes	No	
8. Space for creativity *This factor is characterized by an ability to provide room for creativity and effectively managing the innovation dilemma*	✓		Operations managers may greatly influence this factor at the team, function, or entire organizational level; see Section 5.2
9. Strategy toward innovation *It refers to the strategic selection of technologies and markets as well as planning*		✓	This factor will be mainly dictated by top management. Thus, the operations function will most probably not have great inference on it. However, in some cases, it may provide some input to contribute in the formulation of such a strategy
10. Coordination of a diverse range of skills *This factor refers to the ability of an organization to combine a wide range of specialized knowledge to develop a marketable product*	✓		Since a big part of the role of operations managers consists in effectively managing resources, they can greatly and positively influence the coordination of a wide range of skills as well as to guide them to contribute in innovative ways to improve the performance of operations

Source: Trott, P., *Innovation Management and New Product Development*, 6th ed., Pearson Education Ltd., Harlow, UK, 2017.

5.4 CHALLENGES IN BUILDING A CULTURE GEARED TOWARD INNOVATION AND CONTINUOUS IMPROVEMENT

The discussion presented earlier indicates that both innovation and continuous improvement cultures appear to be attractive options going forward in the competitive domain because of their growing popularity and the advantages they bring. As a result, organizations may be tempted to develop such cultures; however, easier said than done, they may encounter significant challenges. Changing the culture of the department may take a year or so but still relatively easier when compared to changing the culture of the entire organization, which may take years, or even decades, depending on the size of the organization and deeply rooted existing culture. Hence, to bring change in an organization, change management theories can be followed which recommends taking small steps leading to larger improvements. However, we do not intend to discuss how we can overcome the challenges of building a culture of innovation and continuous improvement. This section rather aims to recognize and highlight that the major challenge of building a culture geared toward innovation and continuous improvement is to make the transition from the old organizational culture toward the desired one. Readers interested in reviewing the ways in which organizational culture can change may refer to the works of Bremer (2012), Schabracq (2009), and Alvesson and Sveningsson (2008).

Imai Masaaki, the Japanese quality management and kaizen guru, suggests a three-stage process that organizations normally go through while transitioning toward a continuous improvement culture. These three stages are also well applicable while transition toward an innovation culture. The recognition of these stages is important for operations managers to understand how a cultural change toward innovation and continuous improvement can be achieved.

According to Masaaki, the first stage involves operations managers supporting innovative improvement ideas emerging from employees, no matter how small they may be. Operations managers can facilitate this by encouraging employees and virtually supporting any improvement ideas in order to build the enthusiasm and engagement. As one progresses in the transition journey, that is, moving on to the second stage, operations managers must also develop adequate education and training provisions for their employees such as training on developing problem-solving skills, creative and critical thinking skills, and decision-making skills. These provisions will ensure that employees are able to develop their skills and come up with better quality improvement suggestions. Masaaki further emphasizes that organizations should not be concerned about the return on investment (ROI) at this second stage. Once the employees are motivated and educated about innovation and continuous improvement, then only organizations should be thinking about the returns; hence, this is something to be focused only in the third stage. However, Masaaki acknowledges that organizations often want to immediately see the ROI and payback of the first two stages, instead of focusing on the development of a continuous improvement (and possibly innovation) culture over a span of time between five and ten years. Often this is the transition time period that organizations need for their cultural transformation into a continuous improvement one (Liker, 2004). Therefore, operations managers and their organizations should be well aware that the benefits are only expected in the medium to long terms, and there is no shortcut. This is in line with the first organizational characteristic for innovation presented in Table 5.1.

5.5 ENGAGING EMPLOYEES IN INNOVATION AND CONTINUOUS IMPROVEMENT

We started our discussion in this chapter (Section 5.2) by highlighting the significance of employee engagement in achieving and sustaining innovation and continuous improvement culture. It is a well-known fact that failure to win the full commitment of employees will result in less-than-desired outcomes. As a result, organizations often fail to achieve successful transition toward an innovation or continuous improvement culture if their employees are not committed. Therefore, this raises an important question: How can operations managers gain the full commitment and engagement of their employees to embed the innovation and continuous improvement culture and actively motivate them to participate in the organization's initiatives? Over the years, different strategies and techniques have been studied and proposed by subject experts such as Landes (2012), Albrecht (2010), and Cook (2008). We recommend readers to explore the works of these authors if more detailed information on the subject of employee engagement is sought.

It is evident from the above-mentioned discussions that employee engagement is a complex organizational phenomenon and not straightforward. However, some relatively simple attitudes and behaviors of operations managers can contribute to achieve such engagement, such as demonstrating that they care about their employees and value their ideas in the organization's journey toward operational innovation and continuous improvement. Operations managers, therefore, need to be proactive and continuously communicate with their staff to seek views and to get to know them personally. They should also follow the tried and tested *management by walking about* technique. Readers can refer to the work of Rubin and Stone (2010) for more information on this technique. These behaviors of operations managers can demonstrate their positive outlook toward employees and entrust a belief that they care about them and value their inputs. However, sometimes it may take more time to win over employees particularly who have not been engaged previously by leaders/managers, but here the key is to be perseverant with the same message every day until all employees start trusting their managers and finally come on board.

The continuous effort of operations managers and indeed the top management to show their commitment toward their employees and build trust is a recurring theme in effective and sustainable innovation and continuous improvement initiatives and programs. Therefore, the positive and motivating leadership attitude of operations managers and top management is vital for achieving sustainable results in their innovation and improvement efforts.

5.6 SUMMARY

Despite having technical knowledge and expertise on innovation and continuous improvement—approaches and tools essential for the improvement of operations—developing the right culture in an organization to be able to embark and engage on these activities is equally, or even more, important to guarantee their success. For this reason, we have dedicated this chapter to discuss how operations managers can build a culture of innovation and continuous improvement. To do this, we have discussed the role and importance that building an adequate culture has to support innovation and continuous improvement initiatives, as we all have defined and provided some suggestions regarding how operations managers can develop the organizational characteristics that support innovation and continuous improvement. Here we have emphasized that organizations should not choose from having either an innovation or a continuous improvement culture but to foment the characteristics of both of them as they complement each other. Additionally, we have commented on the main challenges that organizations may face when building a culture geared toward innovation and continuous improvement as well as the different stages that the transition will consist of. Finally, employees' engagement is vital in achieving and sustaining both an innovation and a continuous improvement culture. Thus, we have also provided some suggestions regarding how this can be achieved.

KEY POINTS TO REMEMBER

- Culture plays an important role in, among other things, determining how committed organizations are to innovate and continuously improve as well as how successful they are with these activities.
- Organizations and operations managers must therefore foment the right thinking, behavior, and beliefs (i.e., culture) in their employees and company.
- There are specific organizational characteristics that make some organizations more innovative and committed to continuous improvement than others. These are the characteristics that organizations and operations managers should develop.
- Organizations should not choose from having either an innovation or a continuous improvement culture but to foment the characteristics of both of them as they are complementary to each other.
- To create a culture of innovation and continuous improvement, it is recommended to start with small steps that can later lead to larger improvements, ending in a change of culture. Also, Imai Masaaki's process for cultural change can be used as the basis to transit a culture from not being to be an innovation and continuous improvement culture.
- Employees' engagement is vital in achieving and sustaining both an innovation and a continuous improvement culture.
- In this context, management by walking has been recognized as a powerful strategy to engage employees.

CASE STUDY

Continuous Improvement at FTSE Aerospace and Defence Group

Lefteris Andreadis

Operations Project Manager at Meggitt Plc, UK

The latest definition of corporate insanity is *doing the same things over and over again expecting different results, and expecting to get paid for it*. Operations leaders need to challenge the status quo and encourage employees to embrace change as a critical part of the organization's operational innovation journey. A popular and widely accredited way of applying innovation throughout several types of organizations is by enabling a culture of continuous improvement.

Here a major improvement project in an Aerospace and Defence group's site that manufactures heat exchangers for commercial and military aircraft engines is presented. It regards the transformation of a customer interface cell (CIC), which had been a bottleneck in terms of delivery and quality, among other issues. The CIC includes the end-of-line operations, the inspection process, and packaging, occupying 16–20 people.

Hence, the project definition was to *create a Lean and efficient customer interface cell that is capable of reliably confirming that the products meet the internal and contracted quality and timely delivery standards*.

The overall CIC improvement project was broken down to a DMAIC cycle. Briefly:

DEFINE

During the first stage of the project, the project scope and the expected benefits were identified. Alongside, the required resources were defined and a ten-member project team was created. Project sponsors would be the general manager and the operations director

(Continued)

of the plant, the project owner would be the operations lead, and the rest of the team would be constituted by quality, maintenance, the team leader, and shop-floor stakeholders. Wastes that would affect the company's performance objectives in terms of quality, delivery, and inventory and productivity (QDIP) were identified. Such wastes were excessive process times and waiting times, excessive work-in-progress (WIP), unnecessary motion, rework, incapability of achieving on-time delivery (OTD), and low right first-time (RFT) ratios.

MEASURE

Going forward, the improvement team collected data by investigating the following:

- Processes
- Routings
- Skills matrix
- Required tools and equipment
- Demand and capacity plan
- Supply chain (internal and external)

The team determined KPIs in terms of throughput, yield, on-time delivery, and employee and customer satisfaction. The overall process was mapped out, and motion and times were documented by developing Spaghetti diagrams (Figure CS5.1) and value stream maps to illustrate the current state.

The inspector documented traveling approximately 200 m/unit—this would be due to lack of equipment and tools, which required him or her walking to a different cell to get equipped, as well as the process not being in alignment with the layout. It became clear that the written processes and routings and the current layout along with the available equipment toolset were creating a fragmented and discontinuous sequence of processes in a challenging working environment.

(Continued)

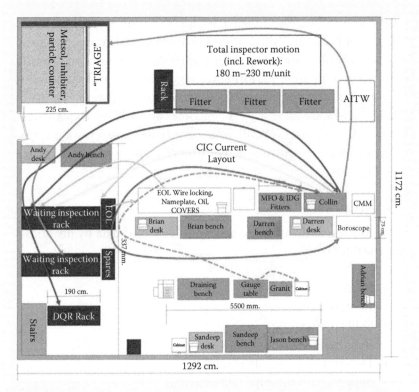

FIGURE CS5.1
Current layout.

Each individual area needed to be properly examined and stakeholders were assigned accordingly, for example, the manufacturing engineer on the processes, the value stream managers on the routings, and so on.

ANALYZE

Before moving toward layout changes, the shown fragmentation had to be deeply understood and redefined. The root causes of the problems were identified in the following key areas and thus needed to be tackled:

- The final inspection procedures and the CIC routings had to be rewritten and rescheduled.

(Continued)

- The inspection process had to be broken down to phases to achieve TAKT time, by delegating resources more effectively, for example, considering a hypothetical TAKT time of 20 minutes, instead of having one inspector working a total of 60 minutes on one product we would change it to three inspectors working on three sequential phases of maximum 20 minutes each and enable a single-piece flow. This required training and redefinition of the skills matrix in order for every inspector to be able to work on every product. Actions had to be taken to improve our RFT ratio from the feeder cells. We were in need of tracking and monitoring mechanisms.
- Actions had to be taken to improve our RFT ratio from the feeder cells. The team was in need of tracking and monitoring mechanisms.
- The layout had to be redesigned and equipment had to be purchased to enhance the process capability.
- A new efficient quality clinic had to be created to enable better visibility and clearing out the space from buffered WIP that was awaiting rework.

IMPROVE

Kaizen events and change management activities ensured that the whole team was on the *same page* and people recognized the need for change. The actions that were determined would be constituted of the following Lean principles:

1. Establish standard work
2. Organize the workplace (5S & Kanban)
3. Create visual workplace (displays, controls)
4. Training and certification
5. Determine standard start position
6. Create a *physical* Andon and rapid problem solving
7. Design the process for flow (Figure CS5.2)—within TAKT time
8. Engage employees and leadership

(Continued)

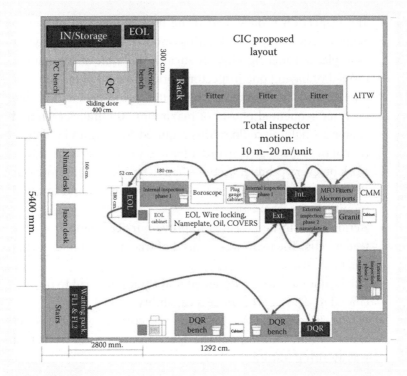

FIGURE CS5.2
Proposed layout.

The successful results achieved can be summarized by the following and complemented by the figures as follows:

- Established a visual work environment with integrated 5S principles (Figure CS5.3)
- Created an efficient and effective, previously nonexisting quality clinic (Figure CS5.4)
- Increased RFT (25%)
- Reduced paperwork issues (>50%)
- Kanban: Better planning and decreased WIP
- Created a continuous, sequential, and efficient flow
- Reduced process times/enabled better resource utilization
- Increased quality and mitigated rework
- Improved responsiveness by QEs and MRB
- Enhanced employee motivation and commitment

(Continued)

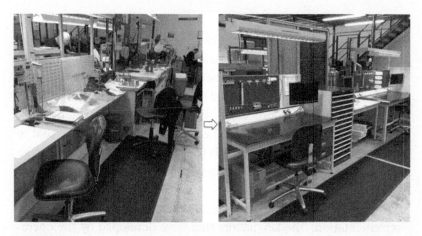

FIGURE CS5.3
Work environment transformation.

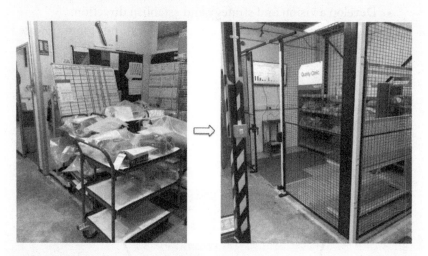

FIGURE CS5.4
Quality clinic transformation.

CONTROL

Sustaining the change is one of the most difficult practices to master. As humans, some of us are not used to walk out from our *comfort zone.* Therefore, we must hold each other accountable to follow the established principles: from the back offices to the shop-floor. Reward

(Continued)

and recognition can be a powerful tool to help with this process. As his or her role indicates, the operations lead needs to be present to supervise the sustainment of the change by demonstrating in detail to every individual stakeholder the advantages that were gained.

The whole change activity could be summarized by Figure CS5.5.

People fear leaving processes, systems, and tools that they are comfortable with and may have been successful with in the past to try new ways of doing things. This fear generally causes people to go through stages or phases of change during which they will behave differently.

The whole project had a six-month duration, from conception to implementation. The key factors that were developed by the operations leader to enable its successful completion were as follows:

- Develop a vision and strategy and establish direction.
- Communication—identify the real issues and communicate the change.

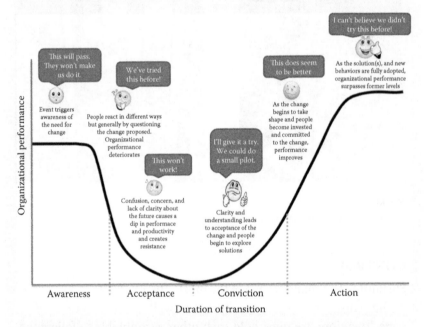

FIGURE CS5.5
Change steps.

(*Continued*)

- Build bridges with the key stakeholders across all the different disciplines.
- Teamwork—constant meetings and Kaizen events.
- Lead with drive, persistence, and resilience.
- Do not let perfect get in the way of better.
- Generate short-term wins.
- Act with a strategic perspective—most pieces must be connected and aligned.

The most difficult issue to overcome was the cultural aspect that was accompanied by people's strong resistance. Even if there is an important reasoning behind every change, most people are uncomfortable with it. In order for any improvement plan to succeed, people—especially those that are directly affected by the change—need to be a part of it in every step of the process. They need to be those that generate good ideas and set the requirements, and the leaders those who connect the dots and prioritize. The operations leader needs to constantly communicate the need for change, exhibit motivation and self-belief, and show that he or she is capable of driving and leading such a major change. I learned that persistence, resilience, commitment, and the ability of bringing people together on the same track effectively contributed in achieving the desired result.

REFERENCES

Albrecht, S.L. (2010). *Handbook of Employee Engagement: Perspectives, Issues, Research and Practice (New Horizons in Management)*, Cheltenham, UK: Edward Elgar Publishing Ltd.

Alvesson, M., Sveningsson, S. (2008), *Changing Organisational Culture: Cultural Change Work in Progress.* London, UK: Routledge.

Bremer, M. (2012). *Organisational Cultural Change: Unleashing Your Organization's Potential in Circles of 10.* Zwolle, the Netherlands: Kikker Groep.

Cook, S. (2008). *The Essential Guide to Employee Engagement: Better Business Performance Through Staff Satisfaction.* London, UK: Kogan Page.

Grover, V., Kettinger, W.J. (1998), *Business Process Change: Reengineering Concepts, Methods and Technologies.* London, UK: Idea Group Publishing.

Haeckel, S.H. (1999), *Adaptive Enterprise: Creating and Leading Sense-And-Respond Organisations.* Boston, MA: Harvard Business School Press.

Handy, C.B. (1993). *Understanding Organisations*, 4th ed. New York, NY: Penguin.

Hope, J., Bunce, P., Röösli, F. (2011). *The Leader's Dilemma: How to Build an Empowered and Adaptive Organization without Losing Control.* West Sussex, UK: John Wiley & Sons.

Jekiel, C.M. (2011). *Lean Human Resources: Redesigning HR Processes for Culture of Continuous Improvement, Productivity Press.* New York, NY: Taylor & Francis Group.

Landes, L. (2012). *Getting to the Heart of Employee Engagement: The Power and Purpose of Imagination an Free Will in a Workplace—A Business Fable.* Bloomington, IN: iUniverse.

Liker, J.K. (2004). *The Toyota Way: 14 Management Principles from the World's Greatest Manufacturer.* Berkshire, UK: McGraw-Hill.

Miller, J., Wroblewski, M., Villafuerte, J. (2014). *Creating a Kaizen Culture: Align the Organisation, Achieve Breakthrough Results, and Sustain the Gains.* Berkshire, UK: McGraw-Hill.

Reigle, R.F. (2001). Measuring organic and mechanistic cultures. *Engineering Management Journal* 13(4): 3–8.

Rubin, M.S. and Stone, R.K. (2010). Adapting the "managing by walking around" methodology as a leadership strategy to communicate a hospital-wide strategic plan. *Journal of Public Health Management & Practice* 16(2): 162–166.

Schabracq, M.J. (2009). *Changing Organisational Culture: The Change Agent's Guidebook.* West Sussex, UK: John Wiley & Sons.

Trott, P. (2017). *Innovation Management and New Product Development*, 6th ed. Harlow, UK: Pearson Education Ltd.

Van Aartsengel, A., Kurtoglu, S. (2013). *A Guide to Continuous Improvement Transformation: Concepts, Processes, Implementation.* Berlin, Germany: Springer.

Van der Panne, G., van Beers, C., Kleinknecht, A. (2003). Success and failure of innovation: A literature review. *International Journal of Innovation Management* 7(3): 309–338.

Von Stamm, B. (2008). *Managing Innovation, Design and Creativity*, 2nd ed. West Sussex, UK: John Wiley & Sons.

FURTHER SUGGESTED READINGS

Cameron, K.S., Quinn, R.E. (2011). *Diagnosing and Changing Organizational Culture: Based on the Competing Values Framework.* West Sussex, UK: John Wiley & Sons.

Horibe, F. (2001). *Creating the Innovation Culture: Leveraging Visionaries, Dissenters and Other Useful Troublemakers.* West Sussex, UK: John Wiley & Sons.

Mullins, L.J. (2013). *Management and Organisational Behaviour.* Essex, UK: Prentice Hall/Financial Times.

Rathi, A. (2014). To encourage innovation, make it a competition. *Harvard Business Review.*

Schein, E.H. (2010). *Organizational Culture and Leadership*, 4th ed. West Sussex, UK: John Wiley & Sons.

Swaney III, P.W. (2012). *Cultural Kaizen: The Story of How Simple Concepts Can Transform an Organizations Culture, Engagement and Bottom-line.* CreateSpace Independent Publishing Platform.

6

Getting the Right Organizational Structure and Working Environment to Balance Innovation and Efficiency

6.1 INTRODUCTION

Innovation activities, whether related to operational innovation or any other types of innovations such as organizational, managerial, process, services, and so on, are multidisciplinary and complex actions that involve several functions of an organization (e.g., manufacturing, marketing, R&D, human resources, and finance), its suppliers, and customers. This is also the case for continuous improvement activities, which are normally *intra-conducted* across different departments and *inter-conducted* with an organization's suppliers and customers. For this reason, and in order for these activities to succeed, it is important to achieve a high level of coordination among all the functions, suppliers, and customers involved. This is facilitated, or hindered, by the way in which an organization is structured. Considering this important organizational element for the success of innovation and continuous improvement strategies and activities, in this chapter, we discuss the importance of an organizational structure not only on innovation and continuous improvement terms but also on the overall performance of a company, the different types of organizational structures, and the difference between mechanistic and organic organizations. In the former, we pay emphasis on the link between the mechanistic and organic structures with innovation and continuous improvement. Finally, since the most common types of organizational structures (e.g., functional) have been widely criticized by business excellence and quality specialists, in this chapter, we also discuss their proposed alternative—in this case, an organizational structure managed by processes.

6.2 AN INTRODUCTION TO ORGANIZATIONAL STRUCTURE AND ITS IMPORTANCE

6.2.1 Organizational Structure

In the previous chapter, we discussed the importance of building a culture of innovation and continuous improvement. Another important factor linked to operational innovation and continuous improvement in an organization is the organizational structure. The way in which an organization is structured has a huge influence on its employees' productivity, which provides them a sense of direction aligned to the goals and objectives of the organization. In simple terms, an organizational structure can be thought of as a pattern of relationships that define the channels of communication that exist within an organization, responsibilities, and tasks of the employees, as well as their relationships and work roles. A well-defined organizational structure eases the process of management and a framework of command and order, leading to effective planning, organization, direction, and control of the activities of the organization. As a result, an organizational structure allows the operations function and guides operations managers to understand what their roles, responsibilities, and tasks are, their relationship with other core and support functions of the organization, as well as the lines of communication that they must follow to communicate (e.g., raise an issue, make requests, and so on). For instance, it provides the direction whether the quality-control activity falls within the responsibility of an operations manager or a quality manager. In most large organizations, manufacturing (i.e., operations) and quality-control activities (e.g., inspection, testing, defects root-cause analysis, and so on) are handled by two separate departments. However, in small- and medium-scale enterprises, mostly they tend to be integrated within the umbrella of only one department (i.e., operations). An organizational structure, thus, provides visual and process clarity over these variations.

It is clear from the earlier discussions that for every organization (whether large/medium/small), a well-defined and clear structure is very important. However, the level of complexity linked to the organizational structure varies for different sizes of organizations. For instance, in small organizations, structures are simple as the relationships between members of the organization, the definition of tasks and authority, and the distribution of work activities are established in a more informal and personal basis. On the contrary, the larger the organization, the greater the need for a carefully planned, well-defined, and purposeful structure. For example, it would be very difficult to imagine large organizations like Rolls-Royce, which employs around 54,000 staff to manufacture and service aero engines operating in over 50 countries around the world, to function effectively without a wisely designed and clear organizational structure. However, one should also keep in mind that organizations are open systems that need to evolve, change, and adapt according to the external environment. Hence, the structure requires a continual review, ensuring their effectiveness for the particular organization and meeting the pace of the market dynamics as well as growth and development of the organization. This is the reason as to why we very often hear the statement *Company X is under restructure.*

6.2.2 Objectives of an Organizational Structure

The objectives of the organizational structure include (adapted from Mullins, 2013 and Knight, 1977):

- Checking and auditing (i.e., monitoring) of the activities of an organization
- Coordination of different functional areas and parts of the organization
- Most efficient economic and operational performance of the organization and the level of resources utilization
- Accountability for the work undertaken by groups and individual members of a functional area of the organization
- Flexibility to respond to future market trends, demands, and developments to be able to effectively adapt to such new environmental conditions
- Social satisfaction of members working in the organization

The objectives outlined above are equally applicable to any organization regardless of their size and the industrial sector.

6.2.3 Importance of an Effective Organizational Structure

The organizational structure is the key to organizational performance. The so-called *founder of modern management*, Peter Druker stated, "Good organisation structure does not by itself produce good performance. But a poor organisation structure makes good performance impossible, no matter how good the individual managers may be." This provides a clear indication that, though the organizational structure may not have a direct influence on performance, certainly it can be considered as a prerequisite to positive performance. Over the years, researchers and practitioners have acknowledged that a good organizational structure improves productivity and economic efficiency, as well as the moral values, motivation, and job satisfaction of the employees. Therefore, a well-designed structure will lead to employee engagement, ensuring a successful transition toward and sustainment of an innovation and a continuous improvement culture.

So far, our discussions have highlighted the importance of designing effective organizational structures; therefore, it is now imperative to pose a question that operations managers need to ask themselves to ensure that they succeed in transition toward and sustainment of an innovation and a continuous improvement culture. Hence, the question would be: How can operations managers design an effective structure in their functional areas that supports a culture of operational innovation and continuous improvement? The upcoming sections will attempt to answer this question by first exploring some different types of structures followed by their linkage to innovation and continuous improvement. Readers interested in further general information and background about the organizational structure can refer to the works of Mullins (2013), Kitchin (2010), Fox (2006), and Martin and Fellenz (2010).

6.3 ORGANIZATIONAL DESIGN AND STRUCTURE

The leaders play an important role in the design of an organizational structure. At the very high level within the organization, normally it is the top management that has the responsibility to design an appropriate structure; however, at the functional level such as setting the operations department, the top management and/or the operations manager in charge of the department agree the type of the organizational structure that would enable the department to achieve its objectives in the most efficient possible manner. Thus, although being part of the broader organizational structure, the operations department and likewise other departments will have their own *internal* structure but that must be aligned to the wider organizational structure. In this chapter, we will pay particular attention to the design of the operations function as we are interested to explore how innovations and improvements in the operations of an organization can be stimulated to support their competitiveness.

When we refer to the organizational design, it is the process activity of proposing and implementing an appropriate and effective organizational structure. There are numerous types of organizational designs that create successful organizational structures. Despite these variations in the designs that create organizational structures, there will be some common characteristics that would enable them to be classified under selected broad categories. However, in practice, they will be enormously different from organization to organization. Some basic forms of organizational structures/designs include: divisional organization, functional organization, strategic business unit, matrix organization, and virtual organization. Different structures have different strengths and weaknesses, and below we provide only a brief review of few structures for you to have a better understanding of the subject so that other more relevant classifications can be linked to the promotion, or hindrance, of innovation and continuous improvement culture. Readers interested in furthering their knowledge on the different types of structures and their characteristics can refer to the works of Ghuman (2010), Mullins (2013), Fox (2006), and Martin and Fellenz (2010).

- One of the forms of the organizational design/structure is *divisional organization*. In this form, the whole company is divided into different divisions that operate as self-contained strategic units, having some relative autonomy from the rest of the organization. For example, Rolls-Royce autonomous divisions include civil aerospace, defense aerospace, power systems, marine and nuclear. In these types of structures, the functional departments (e.g., the operations department) may exist in every division, enabling the division to accomplish its goals.

- Another form of organizational structure is *functional structure.* This is the most traditional and common type of design found in the industry. This structure is based on occupational specialization, where operations would sit as one of the core functions.

- *Strategic business units* or SBUs are separate units of businesses within larger organizations. These SBUs normally have their own mission and set of competitors. Because of their adequate size, it allows them to plan separately from the other entities of the company. An example of an organization having this form of organization structure is the Swiss and food-manufacturer giant *Nestle.* This company has different business units (e.g., coffee, bottled water, other beverages, chocolate, ice cream, infant foods, performance and healthcare nutrition, among others) that concentrate in their own market and with their own team of executives.

- In the *matrix organization*, a project structure is superimposed on the functional structure. In this organizational design, a cross-functional team, comprised of specialists from different functional departments, may be formed to work together on projects that are led by a project manager. This type of structure often comes to existence in the manufacturing industry when, for example, a process-improvement manager (i.e., project manager in this case) is given the task of conducting a Six Sigma project to improve a specific aspect of a production process. In this case, the production manager will carry on having as his/her main responsibility to achieve the targets of the production department (e.g., production volume, efficiency, and so on), while at the same time it may also form part of the improvement team led by the process-improvement manager.

- *Virtual organizations* are comprised of groups of independent people, or organizations, which join together their efforts to render a service to an outgoing activity or execute a project and then dissolve. This type of *modern* organization is only possible due to advances in communication technology, which serves as a basis to form relationships with customers, suppliers, and competitors.

In addition to the aforementioned types of organizational structures, there are many other classifications. But one that is also as popular as the ones discussed previously was developed by Burns and Stalker (1994) during their study of electronic firms in the United Kingdom. They classified organizational structures into two types: mechanistic and organic. These two classifications and their characteristics have been discussed in relation to whether they provide an appropriate environment that stimulates, or hinders, innovation (refer to Trott, 2017). Therefore, these two structures provide a great practical implication for operations managers and their organizations, as recognizing and understanding the organizational structure characteristics that facilitate innovation which will allow them to create an environment to successfully carry out operational innovations improving their processes. The discussions and the implications for operations managers are presented in the upcoming section. However, before we move to those discussions, the mechanistic and organic structures are introduced.

The mechanistic organizational structure is considered as a traditional design commonly found in most of the medium- and large-sized organizations which are underpinned by a well-defined hierarchical structure clearly delimiting jobs and characteristic that makes it somewhat rigid in its functioning. These types of organizations tend to rely heavily on formal chains of command. As a result, they may become bureaucratic, besides usually having a pyramidal structure with a narrow span of control. On the other hand, the organic organizational structure is represented by a more participative, flexible, and adaptable style of management, which does not have a clearly chartered structure. Two main characteristics of organic organizations include a relatively flat structure, with also relatively few levels of management that allow it to quickly respond to environmental changes, and openness to the phenomenon of change and the environment. There are a good set of evidence of organizations adopting the organic structure, for example, Ghuman (2010) provides examples of various Fortune 500 organizations which have reduced their hierarchical levels in order to become a bit more organic. In his study, it was pointed out that IBM reduced its structure from 27 to 7 layers and that Pepsi only has a maximum of four reporting levels. Table 6.1 presents a comparative summary between the main characteristics of organic and mechanistic organizations.

TABLE 6.1

Comparison between Organic and Mechanistic Organizations

Organic	Characteristic	Mechanistic
Must be restricted and uniform	1. Operating style	Allow some degree of freedom
Restricted flow of information, highly structured	2. Channels of communication	Open, with free information flow throughout the organization
Through sophisticated control systems	3. Tight control	N/A
Based on formal line management position	4. Authority for decision	Based on the expertise of the individual
N/A	5. Emphasis on getting things done	Unconstrained by formal procedures
Reliance on true and tried management principles	6. Emphasis on formally laid down procedures	N/A
N/A	7. Flexible on-job behavior	Permitted to be adapted by the situation's requirements and personality and expertise of the individual conducting the job
N/A	8. Loose, informal control	With emphasis on norm of cooperation
N/A	9. Free adaptation	By the organization to changing circumstances
Superiors make decisions with minimum consultation and involvement of company's employees	10. Decision making	Group consensus and wide participation used frequently
With insistence on holding fast to tried and true management principles despite changes in business conditions	11. Reluctant adaptation	N/A
Required to conform to job description	12. Constrained on-job behavior	N/A

Source: Trott, P., *Innovation Management and New Product Development*, 6th ed., Pearson Education Ltd., Harlow, UK, 2017; Slevin, D.P. and Covin, J.G., *Sloan Management Review*, 31, 2, 43–53, 1990.

6.4 LINKING ORGANIZATIONAL STRUCTURE WITH INNOVATION AND CONTINUOUS IMPROVEMENT: A MECHANISTIC AND ORGANIC VIEW

In the previous section, we have reviewed some of the common types of organizational structures as well as the two popular ones: mechanistic and organic structures. In this section, we aim to explore which of the mechanistic or organic structure has a stronger stimulation effect on operational innovation and continuous improvement. There are many supportive arguments in the literature that shows that these organizational structures support innovation, particularly the organizations following the organic structure. However, some authors refuted this claim, such as Child (1973) who argued that characteristics possessed by organic organizations do not support innovation more effectively than those of mechanistic organizations. Nevertheless, this is a well-accepted phenomenon within the business management literature. Evidence also suggests that many of the characteristics of organic organizations are also aligned to and favor the Lean manufacturing philosophy, thus supporting continuous improvement. In earlier chapters (e.g., Chapter 1), we have already established an existent compatibility between operational innovation and continuous improvement. This clearly suggests that in order to encourage the improvement of operations through operational innovation or continuous improvement, operations managers must strive to make their teams, departments, and whole organization as organic as possible. But how can they do this? We discuss some of the ways that operations managers can follow to achieve this in the following:

- Operations managers should aim to *decentralize decision-making*, within their departments. This could be achieved by reducing the formalities and allowing employees to take decisions in situations where they can be considered the experts. For example, an employee dealing with a specific manufacturing operation such as painting the chassis of car should be perfectly able to recognize when the equipment that is being used is not working properly. Hence, for the equipment to be repaired, the employee should have the decision power to stop the whole production line to avoid the production of poorly painted chassis (i.e., defects), even if this implies a significant cost to the company due to production lost. Organizations should be supportive of this decision as there is no point in producing nonconformant products. This decision power given to employees, on the other hand, will instill positive innovation attitude, empower employees, earn their hearts and minds, and engage them in operational innovation and continuous improvement initiatives. Decentralization is also in line with the *automation* principle of Lean manufacturing; hence, this decision will also contribute in creating a continuous improvement culture.

- Operations managers should design *flexible and broadly defined jobs* whenever possible. This will ensure that jobs can be adapted according to the requirements of the situation and/or personality and expertise of the individual assigned to the job. This is another characteristic of organic organizations promoting innovation and continuous improvement. The Lean philosophy anyways encourages creation of multi-skillful workforce by training employees in different jobs.

- Operations managers must also encourage and facilitate *interdependence among employees* that will create team spirit and a positive atmosphere. This will ultimately motivate cooperation among employees in tackling and solving operational problems through the proposal of innovative ideas. A strong team working spirit is also another element highly promoted within the continuous improvement culture.

- Operations managers should focus on *balancing an environment that promotes innovation without losing efficiency*. It is well known that rules, regulations, procedures, organizational planning, and routines are the important elements of any organization in order to ensure that it operates efficiently. However, as we have argued earlier, these will not strongly favor innovation as in many cases, they restrict employees from proposing innovative and better ways to carry out the company's operations because they are *forced* to follow them.

- Operations managers should also encourage *employee initiative and participation in independent problem solving and in groups*. Similar to the interdependence of employees' characteristic, this would promote engagement and teamwork ethics.

6.5 MANAGING BY PROCESSES

As we have now reviewed some most common organizational structures and their linkages with innovation and continuous improvement, we must now explore the importance of managing processes. In the earlier sections, we have identified functional structure as one of the common organizational structures in which a company is organized along functional areas such as sales, marketing, finance, production, and so on. However, the functional structure has been criticized by business excellence and quality specialists who argue that instead of a functional orientation to organizational management, that is, focusing on the activities and performance of functional areas, an organization should focus on managing and improving the *end-to-end* processes that satisfy their customers' needs. A diagrammatic representation of the functional and process management orientation is shown in Figure 6.1.

Process management orientation has greater potential of creating competitiveness for organizations as suggested by business excellence and quality experts; this has also been supported by empirical evidences in literature. For example, the European Foundation for Quality Management (EFQM) model emphasizes on the management of organizations based on processes to achieve business excellence. There are many success stories of the EFQM model such as BMW Regensburg Plant in Germany and

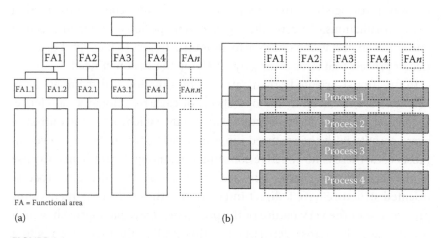

FIGURE 6.1

Comparison between (a) a functional-management orientation and (b) a process-management orientation.

Bosch Tecnologie Diesel e Sistemi Frenanti S.p. A. in Italy have achieved important improvements in their operations due to the process-orientation approach. Hence, operations managers should consider implementing the process management orientation strategy in their respective departments and/or organizations to improve their performance and competitiveness.

6.5.1 Differences between Functional-Oriented and Process-Oriented Organizations

As argued in the previous section, functional- and process-oriented organizations differ from each other where the primary difference in terms of how they are organized refers to the fact that functionally oriented companies are organized in hierarchies where activities are the responsibility of specific units (i.e., departments). Although this commonly leads to a good performance of some functions but often results in poorer integration between them. This is a big limitation of the functional structure, as the good performance or success of an individual unit does not necessarily reflect that the customer need has been satisfied. For example, the 100% availability (i.e., up-running time) of production equipment in a manufacturing environment is assigned of an exceptional performance of the maintenance department. However, this availability of production equipment all the time does not necessarily guarantee that the customer will receive the product on time, with the expected quality and at a reasonable price. In contrast, organizations following the process-oriented structure organize in a different way, favoring structures that permit a strong and constant interaction between functions. As a result, organizations perform better in meeting customers' expectations since the focus is on activities that are part of a particular process that aims at directly satisfying the customer needs.

In functional-oriented organizations, coordination is difficult as many activities are involved in the operations of each functional area. Hence, the management of every functional area must synchronize the output of every activity with the required input in other departments. However, in most cases, there is no effective coordination among departments because of the lack of direct path, whereas organizations following a process-oriented structure have a direct interaction with other departments simply because of the very nature of the process-orientation approach, which occurs naturally across departments. This explicit interaction leads to a direct path for coordination, which subsequently leads to a streamlined and more efficient workflow.

In the functional structure, when optimization of activities is pursued, normally each functional area optimizes their own work and processes independent of other functional areas. For example, if the production department implements an improvement program to increase its production capacity, the other departments such as the sales department may not be able to sell the extra produced outputs due to the lack of coordination between the different functional departments. However, if a process-oriented view is adopted by organizations instead of a functional view, both the production and sales teams would work together to ensure to match the sales figures with that of the production department. This will result in the overall better performance of the organization rather than just the improved performance of individual functional units.

Functional- and process-oriented organizations also differ in the strategic planning. In organizations following the functional structure, targets are normally assigned to the department by the top management based on their functions. For example, the production department receives a target in terms of the volume of production, quality yield, efficiency, and so on, whereas the maintenance department will receive other targets such as reducing mean-time-between failures and total number of hours that certain equipment has been down, and so on. In many cases, often these targets are individual targets of relevant departments without any consideration of other departments. The lack of good coordination between departments often affects the performance of organization. However, when organizations manage processes, the targets set by the management are in terms of the work to be done that spans beyond the boundaries set by individual departments and are based on activities that are part of a process. As a result, departments work together to achieve common targets. We have previously discussed that process-oriented organizations generally achieve a higher level of performance than functional-oriented organizations. Such organizations also present a great opportunity and strategy for operations managers to try a process-based approach on their respective departments.

6.5.2 Transforming Organizations into Process-Oriented Organizations

We have provided a good overview of the differences between managing organizations by functions and processes in the previous sections; however, a key question that needs to be answered is: How can operations managers achieve such transformation? There is no straight answer to this question, as this requires changes not only at an operational level but also at a cultural level. Readers can refer to *Business Process Management* area to further their understanding, and works of Dumas et al. (2013), Weske (2012), Jeston and Nelis (2010), and Smith and Fingar (2007) may be useful. A study by Rocha-Lona et al. (2013) suggests the following phases as the core of successful management of processes. These can be taken as a reference for operations managers who wish to embark their departments or organizations in a transformation to a process-based management approach.

- *Phase I*: During the first phase, operations managers must first identify the key processes and their main characteristics (such as entry and exit points) and also appoint a process manager. Thus, Phase I involves the assignment of ownership as well as the analysis of process boundaries and interfaces.
- *Phase II*: This second phase is also known as the definition phase that involves a thorough understanding of the flow of the process and all the associated activities as well as the facilitation of the communication among involved employees mainly by the process manager.
- *Phase III*: This is known as the control phase that aims at controlling the process and providing feedback to the people involved. Therefore, amendments, corrections, improvements, optimizations, etc. can be conducted if the process is not operating as expected.

6.6 SUMMARY

Since innovation and continuous improvement activities take place across different functions of an organization as well as its base of suppliers and customers, a high level of coordination among all of them is critical for these activities to succeed. Thus, the organizational structure of a company takes a prominent role in this endeavor. It is for this reason that we have dedicated this chapter to discuss the organizational structure of companies, paying particular emphasis on its contribution to the success of innovation and continuous improvement strategies and activities. In particular, we have reviewed the most common organizational structures found in industry. In this respect, we have contrasted the main features of mechanistic and organic organizations. Due to their characteristics and the evidence found in the academic literature, we have concluded that organic organizations are best suited to support innovation and continuous improvement activities than mechanistic companies. Therefore, although we recognize that some mechanistic characteristics are essential to provide an efficient environment, and hence they must be kept, operations managers should aim to develop the characteristics of organic organizations within their companies. This will provide them with the opportunity to create a more suitable and supportive environment for innovation and continuous improvement.

Furthermore, in this chapter, we have also discussed the managing by process approach, which business excellence and quality experts advocate as a better alternative to improve the performance and competitiveness of organizations. As opposed to be managed by functions, this structural approach encourages the definition of key business processes and their management across different functions of an organization. This approach, therefore, presents an opportunity and a possible strategy which operations managers can consider to improve the operations of their organizations.

KEY POINTS TO REMEMBER

- An effective organizational structure is vital to achieve a high level of coordination not only among different functions of an organization but also with its suppliers and customers.
- This coordination is essential to support innovation and continuous improvement activities as they are normally deployed throughout the whole organization, and sometimes involve suppliers and customers.
- Some basic and common organizational structures include: divisional organization, functional organization, strategic business unit, matrix organization, and virtual organization.
- Another widely used classification is that of mechanistic and organic organizations, where the second is considered to be a more supportive structure for innovation and continuous improvement.
- Managing by process is a more effective organizational structure according to business excellence experts, quality experts, and empirical evidence.

- Managing by process simply means that instead of focusing on the activities and performance of functional areas, the organization should focus on managing and improving the *end-to-end* processes that satisfy their customers' needs.
- If an operations manager is setting the operations function and hence needs to decide its structure, he/she needs to consider that this department will be part of a wider structure, in this case, the structure of the entire organization. It is, therefore, necessary for the operations manager to make sure that the internal structure of his/her department is also aligned to the wider organizational structure.

REFERENCES

Burns, T., Stalker, G.M. (1994). *The Management of Innovation*. New York, NY: Oxford University Press.

Child, J. (1973). Predicting and understanding organisational structure. *Administrative Science Quarterly* 18: 168–185.

Dumas, M., La Rosa, M., Mendling, J., Reijers, H.A. (2013). *Fundamental of Business Process Management*. Berlin, Germany: Springer.

Fox, W. (2006). *Managing Organisational Behaviour*. Cape Town, South Africa: Juta Legal and Academic Publishers.

Jeston, J., Nelis, J. (2010). *Business Process Management; Practical Guidelines for Successful Implementation*, 2nd ed. Oxford, UK: Butterworth-Heinemann.

Karminder Ghuman, K.A. (2010). *Management: Concepts, Practice & Cases*. New Delhi, India: Tata McGraw-Hill.

Knight, K. (1977). *Matrix Management: A Cross-Functional Approach to GOrganization*, pp. 114–115. Aldershot, UK: Gower Press.

Kitchin, P.D. (2010). *An Introduction to Organisational Behaviour for Managers and Engineer: A Group and Multicultural Approach*. Oxford, UK: Butterworth-Heinemann.

Martin, J., Fellenz, M. (2010). *Organisational Behaviour and Management*, 4th ed. Hampshire, UK: CENGAGE Learning Business Press.

Mullins, L.J. (2013). *Management and Organisational Behaviour*. Essex, UK: Prentice Hall/Financial Times.

Rocha-Lona, L., Garza-Reyes, J.A., Kumar, V. (2013). *Building Quality Management Systems: Selecting the Right Methods and Tools*. Boca Raton, FL: Productivity Press.

Slevin, D.P., Covin, J.G. (1990). Juggling entrepreneurial style and organisational structure—How to get your act together. *Sloan Management Review* 31(2): 43–53.

Smith, H., Fingar, P. (2007). *Business Process Management: The Third Wave*. Tampa, FL: Meghan Kiffer Press.

Trott, P. (2017). *Innovation Management and New Product Development*, 6th ed. Harlow, UK: Pearson Education Ltd.

Weske, M. (2012). *Business Process Management: Concepts, Languages, Architectures*, 2nd ed. Berlin, Germany: Springer.

FURTHER SUGGESTED READINGS

European Foundation for Quality Management (EFQM). EFQM model, available at: http://www.efqm.org/the-efqm-excellence-model (accessed on August 14, 2015).

Melan, E.H. (1993). *Process Management: Methods for Improving Products and Services.* New York, NY: McGraw-Hill.

Nickols, F. (1998). The difficult process of identifying processes. *Knowledge and Process Management* 5(1): 14–19.

Shukla, M. (2008). *Understanding Organisations: Organisational Theory and Practice In India.* New Delhi, India: Prentice-Hall of India.

FURTHER SUGGESTED READINGS

7

New Product/Service Design and Innovation in the Context of Operations

7.1 INTRODUCTION

The design of a product or service is important for any organization as this activity will greatly contribute to reduce, or increase, in a large proportion, the production or delivery cost of a product or service. For instance, design will not only determine the number of components to produce and assembly, or the number of stages in the delivery of a service, but will also determine their complexity, directly affecting the operations function in this way. It is therefore important to make sure that the operations function provides input at some points during the design stages. Although the design activity of a new product or service will not be directly conducted by the operations function, it is still important for operations managers to understand the different stages it involves and to recognize the fact that they will have to be actively involved and provide feedback during some stages of the design process. It is for this reason that after having discussed some other internal factors, that is, organizational culture and design, that an operations manager will be interacting with in order to effectively develop his or her function, we have now dedicated this chapter to discuss another important interaction, in this case, the design of the product or service. Specifically, in this chapter we review the link between the product/service design and the operations function, paying particular attention to the role of the second on the first. As a general and common knowledge for operations managers, we also review the five different stages that the design of a product or service normally goes through. Finally, since new innovative products or services must be legally protected for an organization to fully take advantage of its innovations, we also provide some general review regarding the importance of protecting an organization's intellectual property and the most common types of legal protections.

7.2 PRODUCT/SERVICE DESIGN AND OPERATIONS MANAGEMENT

We have discussed the traditional role of operations managers in Chapter 1; however, in subsequent chapters we have seen how the role of operations managers has evolved with the changing competitive environment and business models. Nowadays, their role has moved beyond the process-related responsibilities to also expect some contribution in the design of products and services. In any organization, the design of products and services is aimed at improving the competitiveness by satisfying the actual or anticipated needs and expectations of its customers. Therefore, design of products and services play an important role in achieving customer satisfaction. Customer being centric to this drives organization to design products and services considering their needs, requirements, and preferences and creating a specification for the product or service that is used as the input for the operation to create such product or service. This whole process is illustrated in Figure 7.1.

It is noteworthy to mention here that design and invention are two different things, even though in practice designers very often come up with inventions. Roy and Weild (1993) put forward that the design activity is often more concerned with the process of applying scientific and technical principles than inventions. Trade-offs of different aspects that constitute a design are an integral part of the design process. For example, to increase the capacity of an aircraft to carry more passengers the designers will have to compromise capacity with the consequential increase in weight and cost. This will therefore lead to more fuel consumption, will be more costly to run, and hence will be expensive for customers to fly due to increased flight ticket costs.

It is important for the design function and design process to consider the capability of the operation to mass produce or deliver a specific product or service. If the product design does not offer support for manufacturability, that is, if it cannot be manufactured efficiently or even manufactured at all, then the whole purpose of having the best design becomes obsolete. There are numerous examples of design failures, that is, designs

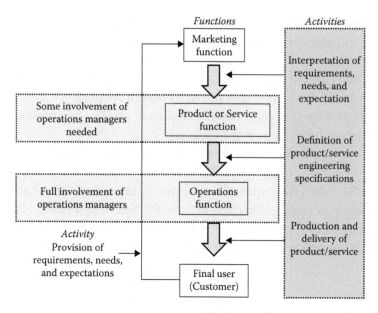

FIGURE 7.1

Process for customer satisfaction. (Adapted from Slack, N. et al., *Operations Management*, 8th ed., Pearson, Harlow, UK, 2016.)

that could not be manufactured. The infamous Tucker automobile case is one of those examples, which is one of the most celebrated failures in the American business history. The vehicle could not be mass produced due to the degree of complexity in its design (Floyd and Spencer, 2015). Learning from these failures, it is important to realize the importance of operations function and hence the role of operations managers in designing products and services. Operations managers' responsibility is to assure that product or service designed can be produced or delivered in full scale and he or she does this by shaping the product through the design process, determining the manufacturing process by which the product will be made, and considering the interface between the product and the people.

7.3 STAGES OF DESIGN—MOVING FROM CONCEPT TO SPECIFICATION

The final stage of the design activity is a fully detailed specification of a product or service. This newly designed product or service serves as an input to the operations function, which will covert this design specification to reality. According to Slack et al. (2016), all specifications comprise of three main elements that include the following:

1. The details of the *overall concept* (i.e., benefits that the design provides, its form, its function, and its overall purpose)
2. Its *package* (i.e., collection of component services and products that are needed to support the concept)
3. The *process* with which the design will fulfil its concept

Figure 7.2 shows the sequential processes comprised of several activities that designers often go through to have the full design ready. However, in practice these processes are not necessarily followed in the sequential form and designers often skip or backtrack through these stages.

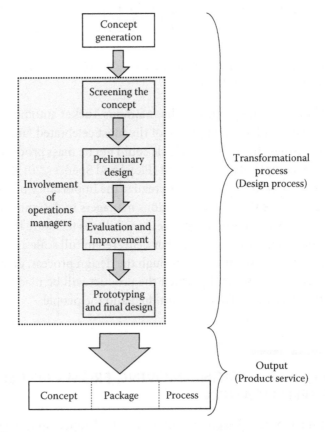

FIGURE 7.2
Stages of the design process of products/services. (Adapted from Slack, N. et al., *Operations Management*, 8th ed., Pearson, Harlow, UK, 2016.)

The operations managers' involvement in the design process varies from organization to organization. In general their involvement is in the screening, preliminary design, evaluation and improvement, and prototyping and final design stages. Operations managers provide input in these stages to successfully manufacture or deliver the product or service. For example, operations managers may decide to run some pilot tests in the production line to verify whether the design favors its manufacturability during the evaluation and improvement stage. In Chapter 8, we will review the design of processes as opposed to the design of products.

7.4 HOW TO GENERATE AND SCREEN A CONCEPT

The first two stages of the design process involve generation of the product/service concept and its screening. The concept of the design of a product or service can originate internally within the organization or externally from customers or competitors. We will now review this in the following sections.

7.4.1 Ideas Generation from External Sources—Customers and Competitors

Design processes within the organization can often be inspired from the ideas generated externally. Organizations rely on their marketing department to constantly monitor and understand the market place and identify new opportunities for new product of service development to meet the needs and expectation of customers. Marketing function follows various formal and systematic techniques to gather this information externally such as the use of surveys, questionnaires, and interviews. Sometimes less-structured techniques such as focus groups and listening to customers from day-to-day contacts are used. The use of less-structured techniques gives customer more freedom to express their views for new products or services as these techniques do not check products/services or test the ideas against predetermined criterion.

Many organizations follow their competitors to seek new innovative ideas that could be translated into a sealable concept, package, and process. Innovative ideas often give competitors a competitive advantage that may compel organizations to follow the same pathway. There are numerous examples to support this and possibly Apple's concept of tablet realized in the form of *iPad* is the best. Apple was the first organization to convert the tablet concept into a successful commercial product, which compelled many other competitors such as Samsung, Lenovo, Amazon, and Blackberry, to follow and offer similar products. The latter entrants in the tablet market simply followed the steps of Apple after realizing the potential that the product presented in the market. Organizations often use *reverse engineering* to understand the development of new products by their competitors to offer a similar product in the market and compete. Reverse engineering helps organizations understand this by moving backward in the product's design process. This technique was widely used in the times of war to understand the defense technologies developed by the enemies. Readers interested to explore further can refer to the works of Raja and Fernandez (2008), Eilam (2011), and Wills and Newcomb (1996).

Idea generation for the new product and services from external sources, that is, customers, or competitors is a specialized area that falls within the boundaries of the marketing function and marketing specialists. Hence, we do not cover this in extensive details and interested readers can refer to the works of Cooper and Edgett (2007) and Garcia (2014).

7.4.2 Ideas Generation from Internal Sources—Staff and R&D

In the previous section, we looked at the external sources for idea generation; however, ideas can also emerge from internal sources. We have seen that the ideas can come straight from the customers but it can also come from the sales personnel's understanding of the market and customers. The direct interaction between the sales personnel and customers provides them with a good opportunity to understand their customers' expectations, which can then be translated into designing new products or services.

In addition to the staff, most organizations rely on their R&D (Research and Development) department for new ideas generation, research, and development. Many large and world-leading organizations spend millions of pounds in the R&D of state-of-the-art products and technologies to remain competitive in the market. In 2013, it was reported that Rolls-Royce spent around £900 million in R&D, whereas other large organizations such as GlaxoSmithKline (GSK) and British

Aerospace Systems (BAE) had spent about £4000 million and £1100 million, respectively (The Manufacturer, 2013). Readers further interested in the brief review of the R&D function of an organization can refer to the work of Trott (2017).

7.4.3 Concept Screening

Once the concept is generated, the next step involves screening them as not all concepts/ideas have the full potential of commercialization. Therefore, designers need to be very selective at this stage and only progress concepts to the design process that are feasible, acceptable, and nonvulnerable/risky. Different criteria are often used as a basis for the evaluation of the concept; therefore different functions of the organization including operations department may get involved in this concept-screening process. A summary of some of the most common criteria suggested by Slack et al. (2016) is illustrated in Figure 7.3.

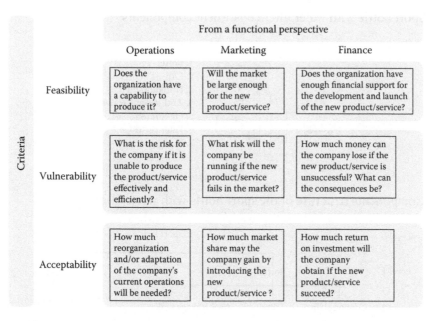

FIGURE 7.3

Common criteria used to screen new concepts/ideas. (Adapted from Slack, N. et al., *Operations Management*, 8th ed., Pearson, Harlow, UK, 2016.)

7.5 PRELIMINARY DESIGN, EVALUATION, AND IMPROVEMENT

The next stage after the concept has passed the screening and involves the creation of the preliminary design (refer to Figure 7.2). This stage aims to take initial attempt at both defining the process to create the package and specifying the component products and services included in the package.

7.5.1 Components of the Package

The package includes the products and services, and specification of these components determines: (1) the constituent component parts that make up the product or service, (2) its structure (i.e., the order in which the component parts must be put together), and the (3) bill of material (BOM) (i.e., the exact quantity of parts needed to make up the final product). This is demonstrated in the below-mentioned table with a relatively simple product example, a sport bottle with water filter.

Sport bottle with water filter constituent components:

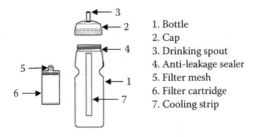

1. Bottle
2. Cap
3. Drinking spout
4. Anti-leakage sealer
5. Filter mesh
6. Filter cartridge
7. Cooling strip

Components structure of the sport bottle with water filter:

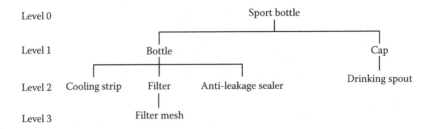

Bills of material for the sport bottle with water filter

Level 0	Level 1	Level 2	Level 3	Quantity
Sport bottle with water filter				
	Bottle			1
		Cooling strip		1
		Antileakage sealer		1
		Filter		1
			Filter mesh	1
	Cap			1
		Drinking spout		1

The above-mentioned example illustrates a simple product with a relatively small number of parts. The three elements of the package definition presented earlier, however, remain the same, independent of the product whether it is a simple product (such as in the case above), or a much more complex product (e.g., an aircraft).

Simplicity in design is normally preferred as in many cases the simplest designs offer the most elegant solutions. However, from operations perspective, the more complex the design, the more difficult it is to produce. The complexity of the design also increases the cost of the product; hence the involvement and input of operations managers in the design process are essential. This will ensure that the designers take into consideration of their input and the product can be manufactured in an effective and efficient manner. Standardization, commonality, and modularization are some of the commonly used techniques for design simplification. A simple example would be the mobile phones where although externally they have different designs and offer different functionalities, many components inside them such as resistors, integrated circuits, and transistors are standardized to same voltages, sizes, and tolerances. This allows the component manufacturers to supply the same product to a wide range of mobile manufacturers, independently of the type of mobile phone they produce. More detailed information about standardization and modularity design simplification techniques can be found in the work of Spivak and Brenner (2001) and Kamrani and Salhieh (2002).

7.5.2 Process to Create the Package

Process to create the package needs to be defined as the BOM, and the product structure just indicates the parts and their quantities that go into a product. This aspect of defining the process is where operations function and operations managers play a major role. Earlier the process design used to be delayed until the product/service design was ready; however this has changed and nowadays both process and product/service design are carried out simultaneously with a strong input and collaboration between the two design teams. For now, it is only important to understand that processes should be at least looked at and considered well before the design of any product or service is finalized.

7.5.3 Evaluation and Improvement

Once the preliminary design and processes have been finalized, it needs to be evaluated and improved before the product or service is taken to the market. There are many techniques available to assess and enhance the preliminary design such as quality function deployment (QFD), Taguchi methods, and value engineering. These techniques are well established and are a subject area itself. There are numerous books and research papers devoted on their application, advantages, disadvantages, and so on. We provide a brief introduction of some of these techniques as follows:

- *Quality function deployment* technique ensures that the product or service designed by organization meets the needs of its customers. This is done by considering the requirements of customers in the initial design phases by capturing *what* the customers need and *how* this may be achieved. QFD is an essential tool for organizations seeking to integrate customer requirements in the new product or service development. Readers can refer to the work of Bossert (1991) and Akao (2004) to gain further insights into QFD.
- *Taguchi methods* also known as robust design methods is used to improve the quality of manufactured products/services. For example, automobile manufacturers test the robustness of car engines by exposing them to very freezing and hot conditions. Although in most of the cases we are not expected to expose our cars to those extreme temperatures, it is something that can happen, remember the unusual

low temperatures reached in the state of New York, United States in 2013–2014. unusual low temperatures are reached in the state of New York, United States in 2013–2014, in such circumstances the car engines should be able to function properly. Therefore, there is a need to build strength in products and services to cope with such extreme situations. More information on Taguchi methods can be found in the work of Wu and Wu (2000) and Fowlkes and Creveling (2012).

- *Value engineering* technique aims at improving the value of products/services by eliminating the costs that do not make any contribution to the value or performance of the product or service. This technique is normally applied in the form of programmes/projects. More information about value engineering can be found in the work of Dell'Isola (1997) and Park (1998).

The discussions presented earlier provide a brief overview of these three techniques and show their contribution to different aspects of the product or service design. Therefore, these techniques can be used concurrently to obtain a cost-effective and robust design incorporating all the specifications and elements required by the customer.

7.6 PROTOTYPING AND FINAL DESIGN

Once the design of the product or service is finalized, the next step involves translating this design into a prototype for testing purposes. This is an essential activity prior to full-scale production or delivery stage to ensure that the newly designed product or service works as per the expectations and meets the quality standards. Therefore, prototype reduces the risks before full-scale production and involves almost everything from models creation to computer simulations. In industries, nowadays use of visual prototyping and virtual reality (VR) simulations to test the newly designed product or service is a very common practice.

The use of computer-aided design (CAD) and computer-aided manufacturing (CAM) to design and manufacture products is a very standard practice in manufacturing organizations. CAD/CAM is used to both design a product and programme manufacturing process in a computer numerically controlled (CNC) machining. CAM uses the assemblies and models, after they have been created in the CAD software, to generate paths for tools that drive CNC machines to transform designs into physical parts. CAD can create any unimaginable modification to a part or product, increasing considerably the productivity of the design activity and also allows the suitability assessment of the design prior to full production. For more information, readers can refer to the work of Rao (2004) and Sivasubramanian (2009).

7.7 PROTECTING THE INNOVATION—INTELLECTUAL PROPERTY

7.7.1 Intellectual Property Protection

Protecting the innovation is a key challenge for organizations. In the previous sections we have reviewed the design process, which in many cases leads organizations to the development of new product or service for the market place. Since the design and development of new product and service could be very costly sometimes in millions of pounds and are a result of several years of research and development, it is important for the organization to protect this innovation legally from being copied or replicated by their rivals/competitors.

Intellectual property protection (IPP) is a complex and specialized area dominated by specialized lawyers, which in most cases go beyond the activities of operations managers. As a result, IPP issues are normally handled by separate department where the issues pertaining to legally protecting the products/services are handled to make sure that competitors do not take advantage of them. Many large organizations such as Apple, Rolls-Royce, and Microsoft, among others, have separate IPP departments. Though, IPP issues are handled separately, it is still important for operations managers to have some general knowledge about IPP as it is closely related to operational innovation and innovation in general. This knowledge will assist operations managers to recognize the creative and novel processes or approaches devised by their organization to improve certain aspect of its operations. If they can identify the value that these new processes/approaches can create in achieving competitive advantage, then they can refer this to their top management or corresponding department to protect them legally from their competitors.

7.7.2 Forms of Intellectual Property

There are several legal ways through which organization can protect their innovations but the most popular and well-recognized forms of intellectual property are *Patents*. In addition to patents, organizations can also protect their innovations through registered designs, trademarks, and copyrights. These forms of IPP have their own unique characteristics and specific functions to assist organizations in protecting their innovations. Table 7.1 summarizes the most common types of IPP and their primary characteristics. More details on IPP for innovation can be found in the work of Trott (2017), Greenhalgh and Rogers (2010), and Van Caenegem (2007).

TABLE 7.1

Summary of Main Type of Legal IP Property, Their Key Characteristics and Criteria

Type of Legal Intellectual Property Protection		
1. Patents	Key characteristics	• Patents provide a 20-year monopoly. It applies to new products or manufacturing processes, or improvements to an existing product or process, which was not previously known
		• Rights are granted only on country filed
		• Patents cannot be kept secret as they must be made public after 18 months of having been filed
		• Commercial value is not guaranteed
	Key criteria	• *Be new*—not made available anywhere in the world before apply
		• *Involve inventive steps*—an invention can say to involve an inventive step if it is not obvious to a person skilled in the art
		• *Be capable of industrial application*—being made or used in industry, must take a practical form of an apparatus, device, product such as new material, substance, process, method, and so on. *Excluded: discoveries, scientific theory, mathematical methods, dramatic artistic work, and so on*
		For example, Penicillin itself was a discovery that was not patentable. However, its process of isolation and storage clearly had industrial applicability

(Continued)

TABLE 7.1 (*Continued*)

Summary of Main Type of Legal IP Property, Their Key Characteristics and Criteria

Type of Legal Intellectual Property Protection		
2. Copyright	Key characteristics	• Provides exclusive rights to creative individuals for the protection of his or her literary or artistic productions • Copyright is difficult to enforce (especially in the *software* and *music* industry) • The duration of the copyright varies according to the description of the work. For example, literacy, dramatic, musical, and artistic work last 70 years after the death of the author. In other cases, 50 years after the calendar year in which it was first published • Copyright does not protect ideas or names. Concepts, principles, processes, or discoveries are not valid for copyright protection until they are put in a tangible form such as written or drawn
3. Registered trademarks	Key characteristics	• A trademark is any sign, which can distinguish the goods and services of one trader from those of another • Registration gives the owner exclusive rights to use trademark, and the right to prevent unauthorized use through legal action • The registration of a trademark is for a period of 10 years and it can be renewed indefinitely for further 10-year periods
	Key criteria	• *Distinctive*—it should not describe in any way the product or service to which it relates • *Nondeceptive*—a trademark should also not attempt to deceive the customer • *Not confusing*—a trade or service mark will not be registered if it could be confused with the trademark of a similar product that has already been registered
4. Registered designs	Key characteristics	• ONLY appearance is protected • Protects for up to 25 years
	Key criteria	• *New*—not be the same as any design already in the market • *Have individual character*—if compared with another published design the differences must make a material different appeal to the eye

Source: Trott, P. *Innovation Management and New Product Development*, 6th ed., Pearson Education Ltd., Harlow, UK, 2017.

7.8 SUMMARY

In this chapter we have focused on discussing the design of new products/services within the context of operations and innovation. Since the design of innovative products or services will greatly contribute to their production or delivery, and hence to the cost of an organization, operations managers should actively participate in it. With this participation, operations managers should be able to provide feedback at different stages of the design process, which must be considered to ensure that the product or service can be produced or delivered in the most effective and efficient manner. Although we recognize that product/service design will fall within the expertise and work of design engineers, and not necessarily operations managers, due to the highlighted importance of involving operations managers in the design process we have reviewed it in this chapter. This will also be the case for the protection of the intellectual property generated through the design process, which will be normally looked after by a legally oriented or specialized function of a company. However, we consider important for operations managers to have some general understanding about the design process of new products/services and how these are legally protected. This would support the traditional activities and contributions of operations managers toward the effective and efficient management of transformational processes and their resources. This is our main justification for having discussed these themes in this chapter.

KEY POINTS TO REMEMBER

- Operations managers have traditionally focused on designing, managing, and improving processes, but contemporary market environments and business models are now requiring their participation and contribution in other areas, such as that of product/service design.
- Organizations must ensure that operations managers actively participate as part of the new product/service design team to ensure that these products/services can be effectively and efficiently produced or delivered.
- Within the five stages that commonly comprise the design process, that is, (1) concept generation, (2) concept screening, (3) preliminary design, (4) evaluation and improvement, and (5) prototyping

and final design, the involvement of operations managers will vary considerably from company to company, but in general terms it will mainly be in stages 2 to 5.

- Design processes will, in many cases, end up producing an innovative product or service that is completely new to the market or that presents some confounding differences with those currently found in the marketplace. Legally protecting this product or service, or its innovative components, will ensure that competitors do not take advantage of the potential investment in cash, time, and effort made by an organization.
- The most common types of legal protections for intellectual property are: patents, copyright, registered trademarks, and registered designs.

CASE STUDY

Product Innovation—Globiaa Drinks Dispenser (www.globiaa.co.uk)

Dr. Tony Anosike

Senior Lecturer, University of Derby, UK

INTRODUCTION

As explained in this chapter, ideas for new products can come from a range of sources—external and internal sources. Internal sources would also include ideas from individuals such as staff members of a business. However, lone entrepreneurs are also a common source of ideas for new products, and the inspiration for specific ideas may be triggered by existing products. Such is the case for the product discussed in this case study, which was developed by the author of this case study. The inspiration for the Globiaa Drinks Dispenser came from the everyday product, that is, globe atlas. This case study chronicles the steps that were taken to fully develop the product—from concept to production.

The first step was to do a quick test of the idea. This involved creating a 3D CAD model of the concept. Although Rhino 3D CAD software was used for this, other easy-to-use free CAD packages include Sketchup, Blender, and so on. It was important that this stage

(Continued)

FIGURE CS7.1
From Globe Atlas to Drinks Dispenser.

is as inexpensive as possible; as a result, it was done by the author. Equipped with the image of the model (Figure CS7.1), feedback was sought from various individuals confidentially.

CONCEPT GENERATION

Once it became clear from the feedback that there was some potential for the idea as drinks dispenser product, the formal steps of product development outlined in this chapter were used—starting with concept generation. In this case, the aim was to generate alternative concepts based on the same idea.

As shown in Figure CS7.2, three concepts were generated with each concept incorporating an ice pack to facilitate the cooling of drinks.

FIGURE CS7.2
Three concept options for Globiaa Drinks Dispenser incorporating ice packs.

(*Continued*)

CONCEPT SCREENING

These three concepts were evaluated using the FAV model (feasibility, acceptability, vulnerability). It is quite clear that although the concept in the second image looks exciting (acceptability), the feasibility of production in terms of manufacturing, tooling, and costs was significantly higher than the other two. The feasibility of making the other two was similar but the idea in the third image has a higher acceptability as it resembles very closely the globe atlas from which the original idea came. So the idea in the third image was chosen for further analysis, whereas the first two were disregarded.

PRELIMINARY DESIGN, EVALUATION, AND IMPROVEMENT

Preliminary design of the chosen concept was carried out using the computer software: Solidworks CAD. With this, it was possible to evaluate the practicality of the design, the fit of the various components that made up the product, and the initial estimation of tooling and unit costs. A number of decisions were made at this stage including:

- *Removal of the icepack*: The effectiveness of cooling by the icepack was analyzed and it was found that in most usage situations, only about half of the surface area of the ice pack would be in contact with fluid. This reduces its effectiveness. The cost implication of including the ice pack was also significant both in terms of manufacturing tooling and unit costs. However, to compensate for lack of ice pack, the *mouth* of the dispenser was widened enough so that ice blocks could be dropped into it.
- *Incorporation of the drip tray within the base*: The drip tray (the shaded undulations at the base of the third image in Figure CS7.3) was designed to be removable but that had some cost implications. Also, removing and replacing the drip tray were not practical in most usage situations. So a decision was made to incorporate the drip tray as part of the base.

(Continued)

FIGURE CS7.3
Preliminary design of the Globiaa Drinks Dispenser.

PROTOTYPING AND FINAL DESIGN

At the prototyping and final design stage, further improvements were made, including improvements to the design and function of the tap. After prototyping, it was discovered that the tap was leaking and hence some redesign was needed to be carried out to fix it and to make it simpler and cost effective. Design for manufacturing was carried out in collaboration with the toolmaker to ensure that all components could be made as efficient and as cost-effective as possible (Figure CS7.4).

FIGURE CS7.4
Changes to the design of the tap.

(Continued)

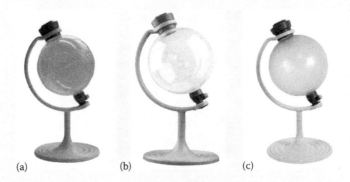

FIGURE CS7.5
Three finish options for the globe part: with (a) landmass, (b) plain/smooth, and (c) textured/frosted finish.

PREPRODUCTION

During preproduction runs, three options were analyzed in terms of surface finish of the globe part: globe part with *landmass*, plain, or *textured* (Figure CS7.5). The globe part finish with *landmass* was the initial idea; however, it became clear that it was expensive in terms of tooling cost and unit cost due to extra plastic materials needed to create the *landmass*. The next option considered was a plain/smooth finish but it was difficult to achieve smooth finish consistently. The third option was a textured finish that gave a frosted appearance. This was the most acceptable in terms of cost and consistency of quality.

INTELLECTUAL PROPERTY

Three types of intellectual property were obtained for the Globiaa Drinks Dispenser: a UK patent, UK and EU Registered Designs, and Registered Trademark. Registered designs require the creation of line drawings to illustrate the design being protected. The line drawings would ideally show all the standard views, for example, isometric, front, back, top, and bottom views. The isometric line drawing for the dispenser is shown in Figure CS7.6 together with the registered trademark.

Further information regarding the Globiaa Drinks Dispenser is available at www.globiaa.co.uk.

(*Continued*)

FIGURE CS7.6
Line drawings for design registration and registered trademark.

REFERENCES

Akao, Y. (2004). *Quality Function Deployment: Integrating Customer Requirements Into Product Design*. Boca Raton, FL: Productivity Press.

Bossert, J.L. (1991). *Quality Function Deployment: A Practitioners Approach*. New York, NY: ASQC Quality Press.

Cooper, R.G., Edgett, S.J. (2007). *Generating Breakthrough New Product Ideas*. Ancaster, ON: Product Development Institute.

Dell'Isola, A. (1997). *Value Engineering: Practical Applications...for Design, Construction, Maintenance and Operations*. West Sussex, UK: John Wiley & Sons.

Eilam, E. (2011). *Reversing: Secrets of Reverse Engineering*. West Sussex, UK: John Wiley & Sons.

Floyd, R., Spencer, R. (2015). *So You Want to be an Engineer? What to Learn, What to Expect*. South Norwalk, CT: Industrial Press.

Fowlkes, W.Y., Creveling, C.M. (2012). *Engineering Methods for Robust Product Design: Using Taguchi Methods in Technology and Product Development*. Essex, UK: Prentice Hall.

Garcia, R. (2014). *Creating and Marketing New Products and Service*. Boca Raton, FL: CRC Press, Taylor & Francis Group.

Greenhalgh, C., Rogers, M. (2010). *Innovation, Intellectual Property, and Economic Growth*. Princeton, NJ: Princeton University Press.

Kamrani, A.K., Salhieh, S.M. (2002). *Product Design for Modularity*, 2nd ed. New York, NY: Springer.

Park, R. (1998). *Value Engineering: A Plan for Invention*. Boca Raton, FL: CRC Press, Taylor & Francis Group.

Raja, V., Fernandez, K.J. (2008). *Reverse Engineering: An Industrial Perspective*. London, UK: Springer.

Rao, P.N. (2004). *CAD/CAM: Principles and Applications*. New Delhi, India: Tata McGraw-Hill.

Roy, R., Weild, D. (1993). *Product Design and Technological Innovation*. Milton Keynes, UK: Open University Press.

Sivasubramanian, I.Z.R. (2009). *CAD/CAM Theory and Practice*. New Delhi, India: Tata McGraw-Hill.

Slack, N., Brandon-Jones, A., Johnston, R. (2016). *Operations Management*, 8th ed. Harlow, UK: Pearson.

Spivak, S.M., Brenner, F.C. (2001). *Standardization Essentials: Principles and Practice*. Boca Raton, FL: CRC Press, Taylor & Francis Group.

The Manufacturer (2013). R&D spending of FTSE-100 manufacturers averages below 5%. available at: http://www.themanufacturer.com/articles/ftse-100-manufacturers-rd-spending-averages-below-5/ (accessed August 15, 2015).

Trott, P. (2017). *Innovation Management and New Product Development*, 6th ed. Harlow, UK: Pearson Education Ltd.

Van Caenegem, W. (2007). *Intellectual Property Law and Innovation*. Port Melbourne, Australia: Cambridge University Press.

Wills, L., Newcomb, P. (1996). *Reverse Engineering*. Norwell, MA: Kluwer Academic Publishers.

Wu, Y., Wu, A. (2000). *Taguchi Methods for Robust Design*. New York, NY: American Society of Mechanical Engineers.

8

What Operations Managers Need to Know to Design Innovative Processes

8.1 INTRODUCTION

For obvious reasons, *product design* has always been a high priority for many organizations. If a company creates an attractive design it not only obtains creative satisfaction and pride from such design, but it can also patent it, which pays off financially. Global successful companies such as Apple, IKEA, Samsung, Swatch, and Nike, among many others, spend billions of pounds creating unique product designs to offer distinctive and unique value propositions to its customers. These organizations have excelled in product design. However, it is less common to hear about companies excelling in *process design*.

Processes enable the translation of unique conceptual designs into real products and services, making the design of processes a key activity not only for the realization of products and services but also for the reduction of operational costs through the optimization of production processes. It also enables organizations to meet the established standards set for its products and services. The need for effectively and efficiently designing processes does not only apply to manufacturers but also to service organizations. For instance, hospitals, bank/financial, hospitality, travel agency services, and so on need to consider the design of processes as a key element of its businesses if they are to offer services that match all the needs and expectations of its customers. It is important to highlight that unlike the design of products activity, which is normally performed by product design engineers, the design of processes is one of the most common activities carried out by operations managers. In this chapter we therefore pay attention to the design of processes. We do this by discussing its relationship to the design of products and innovation, its main objective, and the role of the operations manager in this important activity. We then discuss some of the most commonly used tools employed in industry to aid the design of process flows, the effect of volume, and the variety of products in the design of processes, and the design of layouts.

8.2 PROCESS DESIGN

8.2.1 Interrelation between Product Design and Process Design

The design of product and services was reviewed in Chapter 8, which is often treated as a separate action to the design of processes. However, one should bear in mind that although they are different activities and often fall under the umbrella of different organizational functions, they are strongly interrelated. For example, any changes made by the designer to the composition of a product or service will have large implications for the operational processes that will ultimately produce them. Therefore, it is important to assure that product or service design is appropriate for effective and efficient production. Similarly, a process can limit the functionality of a product or service, resulting in differing looks as expected by the designers. Hence, the process design should meet the design expectation, which is possible when the product and process designs are aligned.

8.2.2 Objective of the Process Design

Similar to the objective of the product design that aims to meet or exceed the expectations of the customers in terms of meeting certain characteristics related to functionality, appearance (i.e., aesthetics), durability, easy to use, and so on, a process design should also meet or even exceed customer's expectations. The design of the process has an important impact on aspects such as the speed with which the product is produced, its quality, and its cost. Therefore, it is evident that both product and process design activities play an important role in meeting the objective of satisfying an organization's customers.

8.2.3 Role of Operations Managers in the Design of Processes

We have discussed the design of products and services in Chapter 7, and pointed out that this activity is mainly carried out by product designers, who in industry are commonly known as product engineers. On the other hand, the design of processes has traditionally fallen within the remit of operations managers. In practice, managers/professionals designing and managing the process are often referred by different titles, besides operations managers, such as industrial engineers, production engineers, manufacturing engineers, and even process engineers. Regardless of the different job titles, they all can be categorized as operations managers due to their involvement in one of the key activities of the organizations, that is, the design of operations, which was discussed earlier in Chapter 1.

8.2.4 Process Design and Innovation

Process design and innovation is a key to organizational success. Hence, operations managers must engage their employees and create an atmosphere encouraging appropriate intellectual activities in order for them to design innovative processes or to improve the existing processes. The atmosphere encouraging intellectual activities will stimulate creative thinking, whereas employee's engagement will facilitate the sharing of the new creative ideas generated from such atmosphere. This will facilitate operations managers to constantly seek the input of their employees in designing new processes or improve the existing ones. This is vital, for example, an employee spending his whole working day assembling car parts in an assembly line would certainly develop an expertise in that area of production and design. Thus, the employee's intellect and expertise should, in most of the cases, be the main source of innovation in any organization. Readers can refer to Chapter 5, where we have discussed in good detail how operations managers can create a culture geared toward innovation and continuous improvement through the development of certain cultural and organizational characteristics, and how they can engage their employees in innovation and continuous improvement initiatives.

8.3 DESIGNING PROCESSES

Designing processes is a crucial activity as they are embedded in all the day-to-day activities of everyone within an organization. As a result of its importance, process design and improvement have become a very important topic of discussion among consultants and the management literature. However, one needs to understand what exactly is a process. A process is a group of sequential activities and resources, which add value by transforming some specific inputs into outputs. A process can be easily visualized in a manufacturing environment as one can easily see the physical transformation of a product. For example, in car assembly process, many parts (input) are put together and assembled (activity that adds value) by machines and shop-floor employees (resources) to produce a car (output). However, this is more difficult to visualize in service (i.e., business) processes where there is no clear vision of the physical trans-formation of an input into an output. For example, in a hospital, patients (input) are examined and prescribed (activity that adds value) by a doctor (resource) so that the patient can become healthy again (output). Therefore, it is clear that processes exist in all types of organizations.

In simple words, when designing a process, operations managers will need to:

- Identify all the activities that are needed to be performed in order for the process to achieve its objective.
- Decide the sequence in which those activities will be carried out.
- Decide what resources are going to carry out every activity.

Designing of processes is not a simple task as operations managers often face many challenges. There are always some constraints that operations managers need to deal with while designing processes, for example, some activities may only be done by certain resources, whereas some of these activities must precede or must be carried out before others. In order to deal with such issues, operations managers must have a clear visualization of the key processes to understand the complexity. *Process mapping* is one of the tools that become very handy for operations managers in designing and visualizing the processes.

8.3.1 Process Mapping

As indicated earlier, process mapping is a very handy tool that provides managers a picture of the overall processes that can assist them to design an efficient flow and management of information and materials, or attempt their improvement. Literature is abundant (e.g., you can refer to the works of Guyer [1998], Madison [2005], Conger [2011], Hunt [1996], Damelio [2011], and Cobb [2005]) with different types of process-mapping tools, each of which has a slightly different purpose. Here we briefly review some of the most commonly used process-mapping tools in industry by operations managers.

8.3.1.1 Flow Diagram

Flow diagram is a schematic or general-purpose tool that is employed to map the flow of material, people, or information. The main purpose of flow diagram is to develop a logical sequence of the activities (i.e., the most efficient order in which they should be carried out in order for the process to achieve its objective) and to show the inputs and outputs between the activities, so that operations managers, or those in-charge of designing or improving the process, can gain awareness of its overall constitution. Figure 8.1 illustrates a flow diagram.

8.3.1.2 Swim Lane Map

Swim lane map is another process-mapping tool used by organizations for general visualization of processes. This tool receives its name of *swim lane map* due to its similarity to a swimming pool with lanes (e.g., who does what). This type of process map has some similarity with the flow diagram but has differences in functional dimension along the vertical axis and a time dimension along the horizontal axis. These dimensions provide information on the phases of the execution of the activities and the involvement of the different organizational functions (i.e., departments) in every one of the process activities. Swim lane map provides a clear visualization of task responsibilities and contributions of every department involved in the process. An example of the structure of swim lane map is shown in Figure 8.2.

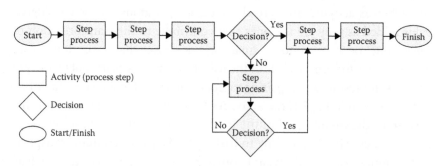

FIGURE 8.1
Illustration of a flow diagram.

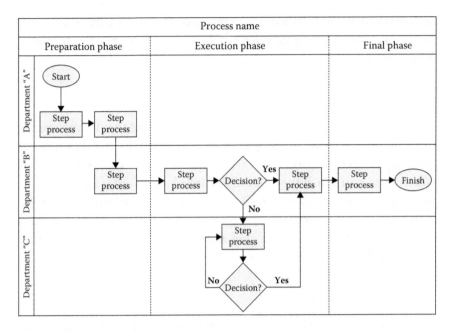

FIGURE 8.2
Example of the structure of a swim lane map.

8.3.1.3 Process Chart

Process chart is a general-purpose table that uses time, distance, and process statuses including operations, transport, inspection, delay, and storage to provide a structured and objective approach to record and analyze activities in a process. This tool allows a clear identification and differentiation between value-added and non-value-added process activities. For example, activities classified as transport, inspection, delay, and storage can be considered either value-added or non-value-added but necessary activities, whereas activities that are classified as operations can be considered value added as they are the ones that contribute to the transformation of the product or service into the final good or service that the customers are willing to pay for. An example of the use of the process chart tool to analyze a process for testing and repairing railroad equipment is shown in Table 8.1.

As shown in Table 8.1, the activities that comprise the process (in this case 26 of them) are listed in the left-hand side column. These activities have been classified according to their type (i.e., as operation, transport, inspection, storage, or delay) and joined by a *line*. Other attributes such as

TABLE 8.1

Process Chart Example of a Testing and Repairing Process for Railroad Equipment

Number	Process activities (Activities symbols)	Operation	Transport	Inspect	Store	Delay	Distance (m)	Value-Added Time (sec)	Non-Value-Added but Necessary Time (sec)	Non-Value-Added Time (sec)
	1st observation / 2nd observation	○	⇨	□	△	D				
1	Go to shelf								6/10	
2	Pick up and take to desk								11/15	
3	Pull up on track it								46/40	
4	Check standards							–	–	–
5	Check notes							–	–	–
6	Identify and open temp								49/69	
7	Identify equipment								10/8	
8	Find blank for results								35/22	
9	Fill job number								26/20	
10	Walk to station								10/12	
11	Setup for calibration								140/190	
12	Calibrate							1071/960		
13	Set off								39/39	
14	Take results to PC								11/11	
15	Input results into computer								74/90	
16	Check cert for details							–	–	–
17	Take to scanner								4/4	
18	Scan								68/41	
19	File test results								189/53	
20	Get results checked and cert signed								41/31	
21	Sign cert on camp?								43/43	
22	Close job								54/50	
23	Collet label								4/3	
24	Walk to table for cleaning								13/12	
25	Remove stickers and clean								351/270	
26	Countersign								44/68	
	Total (1st observation)	2339						1071	1268	0
	Total (2nd observation)	2061						960	1101	0
	Total (Average)	2200								
	% of Total (1st observation)							45.8	54.2	0
	% of Total (2nd observation)							46.6	53.4	0
	% of Total (Average)							46.2	53.8	0

distance covered by the transport operations and the cycle times of every operation, separated into value-added, non-value-added but necessary and non-value-added, are included in the right-hand side columns. In this example, distance was not considered as the operations for this process are carried out in a laboratory, where distances are small. However, for other processes it may be important to record and analyze the distance.

8.3.1.4 Value Steam Map

Value stream mapping (VSM) is one of the very popular tools used by organizations, which can be considered a more sophisticated tool to depict processes. The overall VSM methodology involves:

1. The creation of a current state map that presents the *as is* situation of a process, showing its present inefficiencies
2. The creation of a future state map that presents the *as it should be* state of the process, showing its ideal state
3. An action plan to close the gap between the current and future state maps
4. An implementation plan to put in place the improvement actions to close the gap

A simple example of a current VSM for a company that manufactures parts for cars is shown in Figure 8.3. It is evident from the diagram that process is inefficient due to the existence of a lot of waste. Hence, the process needs to be improved.

In VSM, customer is placed in the top right-hand corner, whereas the suppliers are located in the top left-hand corner. The tasks that comprise the whole process are placed in the boxes alongside some of their specific information including performance data such as number of shop-floor employees per task, cycle time (C/T), changeover time (C/O), availability (i.e., percentage of time that the task/machine is in operation), number of shifts, and task operation time (in seconds, minutes, or hours). In VSM, materials flow from left to right, and this is represented by thin dotted arrows in between the tasks. The triangles shown in the diagram indicate the places where work-in-process (WIP) inventory exists, whereas the thinner arrows indicate the flow of information within a company and between its customers and suppliers. In addition, at the bottom of the diagram a timeline is calculated to show all the waiting times (in this case in days for the WIP inventory) and tasks cycle times in the process (in this case in seconds). At the bottom right-hand corner of the diagram, the total time is shown. Finally, at the top, in the centre of the VSM diagram, the method of production control is presented.

An example of the future VSM for the same process is shown in Figure 8.4. The future VSM that depicts the ideal state of the process should normally be carried out by employees knowledgeable of the processes and the principles and use of VSM and Lean manufacturing.

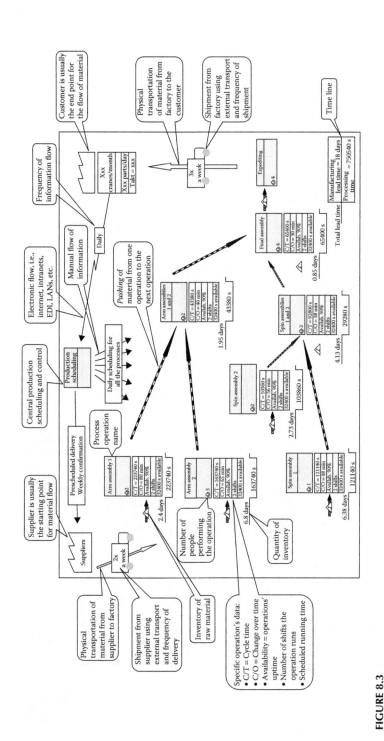

FIGURE 8.3

Current VSM for a company that manufactures car parts. (Adapted from Ferreira, J.C.E., Ristof, K.D., Implementation of values stream mapping in a medium-sized manufacturing company. *Proceedings of the 18th Conference on Flexible Automation and Intelligent Manufacturing (FAIM)*, Skövde, Sweden, 30th June–2nd July, pp. 500–507, 2008.)

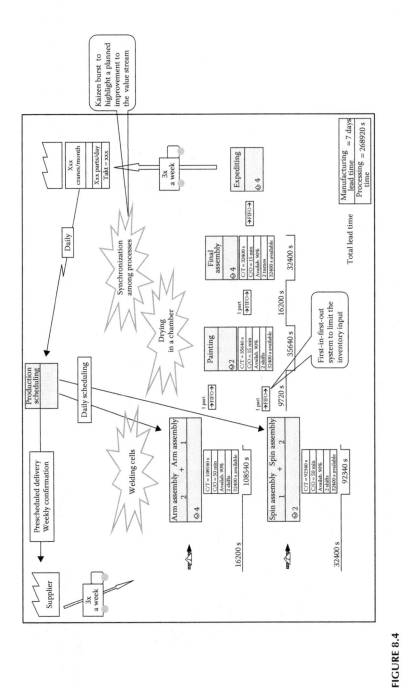

FIGURE 8.4

Example of the future state VSM of the case presented in Figure 8.3. (Adapted from Ferreira, J.C.E., Ristof, K.D., Implementation of values stream mapping in a medium-sized manufacturing company. *Proceedings of the 18th Conference on Flexible Automation and Intelligent Manufacturing (FAIM)*, Skövde, Sweden, 30th June–2nd July, pp. 500–507, 2008.)

The current- and future-state VSM maps as illustrated in Figures 8.3 and 8.4 differ from each other. Some of their noticeable differences are:

- Supplier delivers more often in smaller quantities, from two times to three times a week.
- Production scheduling sends two rather than five information signals (thin arrows at the top of the maps). This facilitates production scheduling.
- Some tasks have been integrated. For example, arm assembly 1, arm assembly 2, and arm assembly 1&2 are now only one task. The same occurs with spin assembly 1, spin assembly 2, and spin assembly 1&2. Thus, resources have been reassigned. For instance, arm assembly 1, 2, and 1&2 were initially performed by a total of seven shop-floor employees, whereas in the future-state map, after integration, these operations are only performed by three shop-floor employees. A manufacturing cell for welding the arm has been created to facilitate such integration.
- A first in, first out (FIFO) system, which ensures those parts that arrive first to the task are processed first, has been implemented.

The changes outlined earlier and additional changes result in reduced lead time (i.e., total time between the start and end of the process including waiting time, storage time, etc.) and processing time (i.e., total effective processing time when the input is being transformed, it does not include waiting time, storage time, etc.); see bottom right-hand corner of both value stream maps. In addition, WIP inventory has also been considerably reduced; see time line at the bottom of the diagram.

Readers interested in gaining further insights into the VSM including its construction can refer to the work of Rother and Shook (2003) and Paton et al. (2011).

8.4 CONSIDERING THE EFFECT OF VOLUME AND VARIETY OF PRODUCTS IN THE DESIGN OF PROCESSES

Designing of processes is an important activity, and two factors play a key role in deciding the type of process to design. Operations managers need to pay important attention to these two factors. The two important factors include the number of products that the organization is expected to produce (i.e., volume) and the degree of variation among these products (i.e., variety). Hence, volume and variety influence many aspects of the design of a process and its future management. These two factors assist operations managers in deciding the type of process they need to design and the approach they will follow to manage them. In the manufacturing sector, normally five different types of processes exist and in order of increasing volume and decreasing variety these are:

- Project processes
- Jobbing processes
- Batch processes
- Mass/assembly Line processes
- Continuous processes

Figure 8.5 shows the relationship of these processes to volume and variety.

The most important characteristics of the five types of commonly found processes in manufacturing industry are shown in Table 8.2. Readers keen to further explore the detailed information about the relationship of volume–variety and its effect on the five different types of processes can refer to the work of Slack et al. (2016) and Paton et al. (2011).

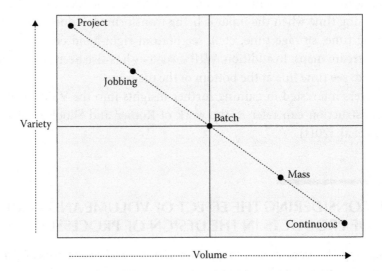

FIGURE 8.5

Process types as defined by volume and variety. (Adapted from Slack, N. et al., *Operations Management*, 8th ed., Pearson, Harlow, UK, 2016.)

TABLE 8.2

Characteristics of the Main Process Types Found in Industry

Process Characteristics		Process type				
		Continuous	Mass/assembly line	Batch	Job shop	Project
Description		Highly standardized products and services	Standardized goods and services	Partly customized outputs to customer requirements	Made to order, custom-made specification	Highly customized and often unique output
Example		Chemical processing industry, oil and petrochemical refineries, beer brewing	Car assembly plant, food-packing process, bottling plant	Machine tool manufacturing, manufacture of most component parts, manufacture of most cloths	Aircraft production, factory built homes, furniture restorers	Shipbuilding, Civil engineering projects (e.g. building a stadium)
Output		Continuous flow	Discrete	Discrete	Discrete	Discrete
Advantages		Very efficient, very high volume	Low unit cost, high volume, efficiency	Flexibility	Able to handle a wide variety of work	Dedicated adaptable team and resources
Disadvantages		Very rigid, lack of variety, very high cost of downtime, very costly to change	Low flexibility, high cost downtime	Moderate cost per unit, moderate scheduling complexity	Slow, high cost per unit, complex planning and scheduling	High risk and cost, uncertainty, takes time to establish
Cost per unit		Low	Low	Moderate	High	Very high
Longevity of process		Ongoing and indefinite	Ongoing for whole product life cycle	Short individual deliveries—repeated often	Fix duration—short to medium	Fix duration—medium to very long
Probable type of layout		Product-service dominant	Product-service dominant	Process dominant	Work cell	Fixed position
Equipment used		Dedicated	Dedicated	General purpose	General purpose	Varied
Skills of labor		Low to high	Low	Moderate	High	Low to high
Work-in-process inventory		Low	Low	Medium to high	High	Varied

Source: Paton, S. et al., *Operations Management*, McGraw-Hill, Berkshire, UK, 2011.

8.5 LAYOUT DESIGN

Process design is critical as we have discussed in earlier sections; however, another important and indeed critical factor that operations managers need to deal with when designing processes is the design of the layout of the physical space where the processes will operate. Layout design significantly contributes to the long-term efficiency of the process. For example, poorly designed layouts can create confusion over long-flow patterns of products or services, whereas they are being transformed, resulting in longer production times, inflexible operations, building up of inventory, and consequently higher costs. Therefore an effective layout design is critical for operations managers. Modification of layouts at a later stage in most of the cases is difficult and expensive; hence organizations are reluctant to do it very often.

Layout design decisions are mostly related to the best and most efficient location of machines in a factory's shop floor (in a manufacturing environment), or offices and desks (in an office environment), or service centres (in department stores, hospitals, or government offices). However, the key question that operations managers face is: How to take the best decision regarding the most efficient location of resources (e.g., machines in a factory's shop floor) to support an efficient process? In this regard, Slack et al. (2016) suggest operations managers to follow a three-stage process as follows:

- *Stage 1*: In the first stage, considering the volume and a variety of products that an organization needs to produce, operations managers need to take decision regarding what type of process (e.g., project, jobbing, batch, mass/assembly line, or continuous) he or she should be designed. The type of process to be designed should be of significant importance as process types and layout types keep a close relationship, that is, some layout types are better suited to some specific process types than others.
- *Stage 2*: Once the decision on the type of process design has been taken in the first stage, the second stage focuses on decision regarding the type of basic layout required. Slack et al. (2016), Paton et al. (2011), and Hill and Hill (2012) considered that there are four basic types of layouts: fixed position layout, process/functional layout, cell layout, and product layout. Table 8.3 provides a brief description of

TABLE 8.3

Main Types of Layout Designs and Some of Their Characteristics

Layout Characteristic	Fixed Position	Layout Type		
		Process/Functional	Cell	Product
Illustration				
Description	Activities are clustered around the product or service to be delivered. Thus, transforming resources (e.g. equipment, machinery, and people) move as necessary, not the trans-formed resource (i.e. output)	Similar transforming resources (e.g. equipment, machinery and people) are located together	All the transforming resources (e.g. equipment, machinery and people) are located together (i.e. in a cell) to meet the processing requirements	The transformed resources flow along a line of processes. Thus, this layout involves locating the resources making the transformation of the product entirely for the convenience of the transformed resource
Type of processes suited for	Project and jobbing	Jobbing and batch	Batch and mass/assembly line	Mass/assembly line and continuous

(Continued)

TABLE 8.3 (*Continued*)

Main Types of Layout Designs and Some of Their Characteristics

Layout Characteristic	Fixed Position	Process/Functional	Cell	Product
Example	Motorway construction, shipbuilding, and construction site	Machining parts for cars, aircrafts, and so on, and supermarket	Manufacture of some components, maternity unit in a hospital, repair shops for items returned under warranty	Assembly of automobiles, most types of manufacturing assembly, bottling an canning processes
Advantages	• High product mix flexibility • Movement of products is minimized • Staff's tasks are of high variety	• High product and mix flexibility • Easy to supervise • Can cope with disruptions and equipment failures due to its robustness	• Smoother product flow and shorter travel distance • Fast lead time and throughput • Minimization of setups • Employees work in group, which can result in improved motivation	• High volume at low cost • Opportunities for specialization of equipment
Disadvantages	• Movement of labor, machinery, and equipment is needed • Cost per unit may increase due to mobile equipment • A problem can be present in terms of storage space and its scheduling	• Routing of the product is commonly complex • High work-in-process likely • Complex flow of the product	• May need more space • May be expensive to rearrange from the existing layout	• Low mix flexibility is likely • Lack of robustness to cope with disruptions • Work can be very repetitive and hence demotivating for employees

the main characteristics of each of these four types of layouts. The choice of the process design leads to the selection of the appropriate type of layout. For example, if an operations manager requires a mass/assembly line or continuous process due to the volume and variety of products that needs to be produced, then a product layout will be the most appropriate type of layout to choose (see the last row in Table 8.3). The relationship between the type of process and type of layout design as illustrated by Slack et al. (2016) is shown in Figure 8.6.

• *Stage 3*: The third and the final stage consists of decision regarding the detailed design of the layout once the process and layout have been decided. In order to make this decision, operations managers must take into consideration criteria such as length and clarity of flow, staff conditions, inherent safety, coordination of management, log terms flexibility, and use of space. The design of layout is a complex area with its own literature and numerous specific techniques such as combinational complexity, flow record charts, relationship charts, heuristic procedures, cluster analysis, and production and flow analysis, among many others. Readers interested in furthering their insights regarding the detailed design of the layout can refer to the work of Hiregoudar (2007), Phillips (1997), and Greene (2011). The books written by Slack et al. (2016) and Paton et al. (2011) can also be used as a good general reference though they are not specialized books on layout design.

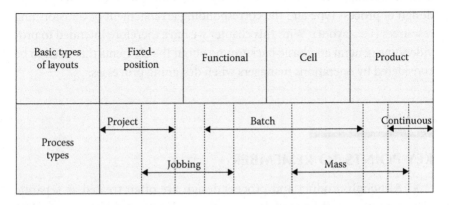

FIGURE 8.6
Relationship between process type and layout type. (Adapted from Slack, N. et al., *Operations Management*, 8th ed., Pearson, Harlow, UK, 2016.)

8.6 SUMMARY

This chapter has been dedicated to review one of the fundamental activities of operations managers, in this case, the design of processes. It is important for organizations to recognize the essential nature of this activity for several reasons. One of this is the positive effect that efficiently designed processes have on the reduction of operational costs in all types of organizations. Another reason is the contribution that processes have to the achievement of customer satisfaction, especially in the service sector where the customer itself is literally the transformed resource by going through certain business processes. Also, as we have been discussing it since Chapter 7, there is a close interrelation between products/services and the processes that make and provide them. Thus, design of products and processes activities must be developed with constant feedback and input from both sides. This critical issue is something that we have discussed and re-emphasized in this chapter once more.

In this chapter we have also established the fact that operations managers will most certainly face constraints and limitations with transforming resources when designing processes, and hence we have briefly reviewed some of the most commonly used tools in industry that facilitate the design of processes. In this case, different types of process-mapping tools (e.g., flow diagrams, process chart, swim lane maps, VSM) can help operations managers understand the complexity of processes and some of its main characteristics, one of them being their flow. We have also discussed the relationship between process variety and volume and their effect on the design of process type and the corresponding arrangement of transforming resources (i.e., layout). With this chapter we have therefore intended to provide some general and basic background about the elements that need to be considered by operations managers when designing processes.

KEY POINTS TO REMEMBER

- Although product and process design are often treated as separate activities, and hence fall under the umbrella of different organizational functions, they are strongly interrelated as even small modifications made to the composition of a product or service will have large implications for the operational processes that will produce them.

- Processes will have a significant effect on the speed, quality, cost, dependability, and flexibility with which a product or service is produced.
- In industry, professionals with the titles of, for example, operations manager/engineer, industrial engineer, production engineer, manufacturing engineer, or process engineer may be the one in charge of designing the company's processes.
- Processes are groups of sequential activities and resources, which add value by transforming some specific inputs into outputs. The visualization of processes is easier in the manufacturing industry than in the services due to the tangibility of manufactured products.
- Processes consist of activities, sequences, and resources that will do the activities.
- One of the tools that are most commonly used by operations managers to design processes and understand their complexity and the flow/sequence characteristic is process mapping.
- There are different types of mapping tools, with the best known being: flow diagram, swim lane map, process chart, and value stream map.
- Process types are defined based on the volume and variety of the products they produce or services they provide.
- Process types include: project, jobbing, batch, mass, and continuous.
- A critical factor in the design of processes is the design of the layout of the physical space where the process will operate.
- Layouts have a significant contribution to the long-term efficiency of the process, and these are linked to the type of process.
- Common layouts include: fixed-position, functional, cell, and product.

REFERENCES

Cobb, C.G. (2005). *Enterprise Process Mapping: Integrating Systems for Compliance and Business Excellence*. Milwaukee, WI: American Society for Quality, Quality Press.

Conger, S. (2011). *Process Mapping and Management*. New York, NY: Business Expert Press.

Damelio, R. (2011). *The Basics of Process Mapping*, 2nd ed. Boca Raton, FL: Productivity Press.

Ferreira, J.C.E., Ristof, K.D. (2008). Implementation of values stream mapping in a medium-sized manufacturing company. *Proceedings of the 18th Conference on Flexible Automation and Intelligent Manufacturing (FAIM)*, Skövde, Sweden, 30th June–2nd July, pp. 500–507.

Greene, J. (2011). *Plant Design, Facility Layout, Floor Planning.* Charleston, SC: CreateSpace Independent Publishing Platform.

Guyer, H.H. (1998). *Industrial Processes and Waste Stream Management.* West Sussex, UK: John Wiley & Sons.

Hill, A., Hill, T. (2012). *Operations Management*, 3rd ed. London, UK: Palgrave Macmillan.

Hiregoudar, C. (2007). *Facility Planning and Layout Design.* Pune, India: Technical Publications Pune.

Hunt, V.D. (1996). *Process Mapping: How to Reengineer Your Business Processes.* West Sussex, UK: John Wiley & Sons.

Madison, D. (2005). *Process Mapping, Process Improvement, and Process Management: A Practical Guide to Enhancing Work and Information Flow.* Chico, CA: Paton Press.

Paton, S., Clegg, B., Hsuan, J., Pilkington, A. (2011). *Operations Management.* Berkshire, UK: McGraw-Hill.

Phillips, E.J. (1997). *Manufacturing Plant Layout: Fundamentals and Fine Points of Optimum Facility Design.* Dearborn, MI: Society of Manufacturing Engineers.

Rother, M., Shook, J. (2003). *Learning to See: Value Stream Mapping to Create Value and Eliminate Muda.* Cambridge, MA: Lean Enterprise Institute.

Slack, N., Brandon-Jones, A., Johnston, R. (2016). *Operations Management*, 8th ed. Harlow, UK: Pearson.

9

Innovation and Sustainability

9.1 INTRODUCTION

In earlier chapters, we explored various dimensions of innovation, from external to internal contexts, whereby operations managers should understand for better planning, designing, executing, and controlling business operations. This chapter will examine one popular and crucial term that operations managers must be made aware of and the knowledge of which to be mastered, so as to stay in line with the recent market focus, movement, and requirement, which is *sustainability*. Achieving sustainable operations would be the goal of any operations manager to meet the corporation's sustainability agenda.

Sustainability has been a buzz word for quite some time for industry as well as academia. So, what does sustainability actually mean and what does it do? What is the ultimate outcome? What impact does it bring and its synergy with innovation? More specifically, why operations managers have to bother with sustainability initiatives and what are the focuses within their role in this context help to design and achieve innovative and sustainable operations? This chapter tends to address these questions and stirs their views and approaches in achieving what is required in the market under the current business dynamic environment and the increasing pressure, externally as well as internally, to be sustainable.

9.2 THE DEVELOPMENT OF SUSTAINABILITY IN OPERATIONS MANAGEMENT

Despite the fact that the term *sustainability* is rather popular in recent years, its idea could be traced back to 1987 during the United Nations conference with the Brundtland Commission's Report, which defined sustainable development as "The development that meets the needs of the present without compromising the ability of the future generations to meet their own needs" (WCED, 1987).

Since then, a few variants of definitions of sustainability in different contexts by different operations improvement gurus have been introduced and it could be confusing for many operations managers as well as academics. For this chapter, we focus on the practicality and the contexts, which are important for operations managers. One should acknowledge that sustainability has three pillars of focuses, also known as triple bottom line (TBL), which was first introduced by John Elkington, a British consultant, in 1994. These pillars are referring to dimensions of social, environmental, and economic, as called the *SEE* dimensions (Figure 9.1), which also sometimes is referred to as 3P: people (social), planet (environment), and profit (economic). Therefore, a true sustainability is an integrated, balanced achievement of these three dimensions in any operation that an organization conducts. Although in reality, quite often more focus has been placed on the economic aspect (e.g., reducing use of materials/resources hence reducing costs), and followed by the environmental (e.g., reducing greenhouse gases emissions) and the social (e.g., improving well-being of operators) aspects. Therefore, as much as businesses want to make more profits (economic), environmental and social aspects must also be

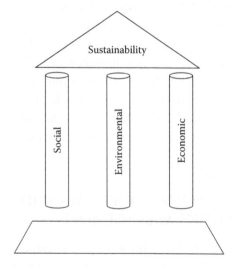

FIGURE 9.1
Three pillars of sustainability.

adequately and concurrently addressed—which is why sustainability is a critical agenda in the modern business environment.

However, one must be clear that sustainability is not another term for corporate social responsibility nor environmental friendliness. Neither it is merely about reducing wastes, increasing the use of recycled materials, recovering recyclable materials at the end of product life cycle, remanufacturing, reducing CO_2 emissions, or simply being *green* in operations, which tends to be the, or natural interpretation among the practitioners as sustainability is concerned.

A few drivers, such as business pressures, resource scarceness, and government legislations (resulting from higher than ever environment pollutions and global warming arguments), have contributed to the motivation of achieving true sustainability. As sustainability has received an increasing attention from organizations of various sectors in recent years, the trend has also become clearer when more and more manufacturers adopt greener processes and management systems aim to achieve sustainability (Klewitz and Hansen, 2014). However, the diversification of implementation approaches becomes a handle for more efficient and smoother implementation. A survey report by Burnes (2003) stated between 40% and 70% of sustainability change initiatives failed. Given that the research was conducted prior to 2003, since then much efforts have been put in by researchers and practitioners attempted to address various technical and operational challenges faced when implementing sustainability (e.g., Law and Gunasekaran, 2012, Vom Brocke, et al. 2012, and among others), the challenges of which include the following:

- Unclear and insensible (and misalignment of) goals
- Lack of management support
- Lack of proper communication channels
- Lack of efficient engagement approaches
- Lack of sustainability standards and regulations
- Inappropriate existing roadmaps, frameworks, and systems
- Inappropriate performance indicators
- Unclear relationship and influence between the three sustainability dimensions in the operations practices

This suggests that great knowledge has been established over the years based on survey and research to make sustainability adoption easier, which is rather crucial for operations managers and the understanding of what sustainability actually means for them and their roles in designing and monitoring operations/processes. Further suggested readings listed at the end of this chapter could be pursued for more details on the principles and practices of sustainability.

As operations strategy and management focus on monitoring cost and performance, benchmarking, outsourcing, managing information and communication, security and safety, and others, and its decisions in product and service designs affect the use of materials and other resources required, both in long term and short term, operations managers' role is well placed to ensure sustainability is well practiced.

Figure 9.2 illustrates the importance of operations managers in achieving sustainability initiatives. The traditional approach of resources/materials utilization results in high disposal of materials (end-of-life's products) to the landfill and very little efforts in designing products by avoiding the use of unnecessary resources and seeking opportunity to reduce, reuse, recycle, or recover energy from any resources. This traditional approach is still to be seen today in some existing business practices. Putting on the sustainability's hat, the triangle of this trend can be reversed and transformed as shown in Figure 9.2 by investing the upmost effort in avoiding the use of unnecessary materials, for example, through better product designs, or can be replaced with more sustainable materials for a start. Eventually, the need for disposal will be significantly reduced. This does not only meet the economic agenda (by reducing the cost of materials) but also the environmental (i.e., reducing waste of materials) and social (i.e., reducing the needs of waste/hazardous disposal handling) aspects of sustainability.

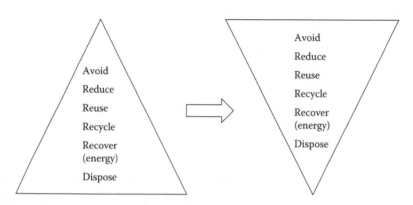

FIGURE 9.2
Transforming traditional approach of business practices.

9.3 THE EXISTING INITIATIVES IN ACHIEVING SUSTAINABILITY

The trend of transforming business practices toward sustainability is taking place and different kinds of initiatives have been explored end employed. Sustainability is becoming a core focus and has been the backbone for many organizations to (re)develop operations strategies and design/planning/control of operations. In practice, operations management involves planning and control, and operations strategy would normally be cascaded, forming the typical hierarchical levels, that is, strategic, tactical, and operational. Planning activities normally take place more at strategic and tactical levels, whereas control activities tend to be at tactical and operational levels. There are also segregations in terms of operation functions across organization. Rushton et al. (2014) proposed a planning and control cycle whereby once we know where we are today, we could set a list of objectives what we want to achieve and then we could start making a plan about how to achieve, and the last cycle is to monitor (which involved control). This planning and control cycle can be applied in all levels and all functions. Similarly, sustainability initiatives and targets should also be deployed at each of the hierarchical levels and within the associated planning and control activities.

Different sustainability initiatives can be observed in different operation functions, for example, human resource, marketing, IT, business performance indexing/reporting, procurement, supplier selection, project management, production, logistics and distribution, and so on. Some existing tools have been used as a means to improve operations with sustainability focus. For instance, balanced scorecards, which is a strategic planning and management tool, has been employed to align business operations to the corporate vision with sustainability agenda and the strategic goals of which have included some sustainability targets. Supply chain operations reference (SCOR) model is a unified framework that connects business operations, people, and performance metrics to satisfy customer's requirement, which include plan, source, make, deliver, and return. This model can be used to analyze the current state of the company processes and to set a new set of metrics for supply chain/company performance with sustainability targets. Other existing tools, such as Business Process Re-engineering, Lean, Six Sigma, have also been used by setting new sustainability agenda. Furthermore, continuous improvement tools such as define, measure, analyze, improve, and control (DMAIC) are also a popular tool to ensure the sustainability is achieved and quantified. We also begin to see environment and social accounting to take form, and with sustainability accounting and reporting tool on its way to be more widely accepted and deployed. In the research community, many have proposed their framework for sustainability implementation, for example, Garcia et al. (2016), Simas et al. (2013), Galbreath (2009), and Carter and Rogers (2008). However, these frameworks are still in research or infancy stage and yet need to be validated further.

Here, we can rightly say that there are sustainability initiatives and tools in place but are in segregation within the organization, and hence, the full impact of sustainability initiatives may not have been fully realized. On the other hand, this could be viewed as enterprise resource planning (ERP) systems that a total one-off implementation for the entire organization will not be possible due to the magnitude of change and work involved.

Bear in mind that each of the hierarchical levels will face different challenges of changes and the operations managers should also keep track of fulfilling the true integration of the three dimensions of sustainability. At the same time, new opportunity of all types could come to light, and therefore, operations managers must be attentive to make sure the opportunity is realized.

It is worth knowing that, as reported by Forbes, BMW was ranked first by Corporate Knights as the world's most sustainable company*. BMW achieved outstanding scores for *efficient use of water, energy, and lack of waste*, as well as its *responsible approach to paying taxes, large innovation investments, low employee turnover, and low CEO-to-average-worker pay ratio*. Once we observe in more detail, the winning elements touched on the three aspects of sustainability as discussed earlier. Corporate Knights measured a company's environmental responsibility via their energy and water use, emissions, and waste generated, whereas for social aspect (i.e., employee management practices), reports of fatalities/lost time, staff turnover, diversity in leadership, and female representation in management/board position were considered. As for a company's financial sustainability, it took into account the revenue generated, earnings before interest, tax, depreciation, and amortization, and the ratio of CEO

---

* http://www.forbes.com/sites/kathryndill/2016/01/22/the-worlds-most-sustainable-companies-2016/#5beef765965f

compensation to the average employee's compensation was taken into consideration. We could learn from this that these measurements are not something new in assessing performance indicators in these three dimensions, but with the sustainability's hat on, there will be meaningful connection between the different dimensions. This could form a foundation for initiatives to quantity sustainability and hence could provide a platform in achieving true sustainability.

9.4 THE SYNERGY BETWEEN INNOVATION AND SUSTAINABILITY

Based on the definitions of innovation and sustainability alone, it is difficult to establish a systematic link between them, whereby innovation focuses on the characteristics and sustainability on dimensions. However, when we take the defining characteristics of innovation, such as newness, significance of improvement, magnitude of change, and commercial value, we can observe the connection and synergy between the two through the activities from both initiatives. For example, one sustainably designed product is seen to be innovative because of its changes made for improvement, newness, and very likely, commercially valued. However, one newly developed innovative product may not be adhering to the sustainability's principles but it is innovative due to its features. In other words, this suggests that achieving sustainability in itself is innovation.

Innovation needs to be sustainable, not to mention the pressures as discussed earlier. We have seen some innovative products are in fact not as good as their predecessors; giving some sustainability thinking and design will improve innovation. Here, we build on the innovation discussion in Chapter 1 by adding the sustainability agenda during innovation process, which helps to address the increasing business pressures and legislations on this topic. Bearing this thought at the beginning of any product/process development process would be an advantage, and it ensures the reap of benefits as discussed earlier. For instance, product innovation and process innovation that were discussed in Chapter 1 are both involving design innovation. If the sustainability focus has been right, in the environmental dimension, product innovation will involve the use of sustainable/recyclable materials to reduce waste and landfills and compact packaging design with reduced materials use, whereas process innovation will promote renewable energy (e.g., solar power) and redesign processes leading to more productivity rather than unproductive repetitive jobs for the workers (social dimension). Furthermore, sustainable innovation will lead to sustainable performance improvement, and in turn will gain benefit financially (economic dimension).

9.5 THE POTENTIAL OF INNOVATION ACHIEVING SUSTAINABLE OPERATIONS

The operations managers must bear in mind the three key dimensions of sustainability, that is, social, environment, and economic. While as much as the organization is striving to maximize their financial gains, they must also take the corporate responsibility toward the environment and social's well-being. The sustainability agenda must be applied in everything an organization does.

In Chapter 1, we discussed that innovation can be radical or continuous and its type includes organizational, managerial, operational, process, service, product, and commercial/marketing innovation. We also illustrated that being innovative in one area will bring impact on the others. Similarly, sustainability agenda is the same, while practising sustainability across the organization, the actions are associated across the three dimensions. For example, if the effort is to minimize the energy used during the production stage by improving the manufacturing processes, this will result in using less natural resources (ticking the environment box) and reserving the energy for the public (social), and furthermore, this will help to reduce the production running cost (hence, economic advantage).

In the preceding section, we discussed the synergy between innovation and sustainability and we can remark that sustainable innovation is a key to achieve sustainable operations. Here, we will reassess the five performance measurements discussed in Chapter 4 with sustainability agenda as depicted in Figure 9.3. This aims to inspire operations managers to consider the three sustainability dimensions in each operation designed to achieve high and yet sustainable performance. For instance, while considering the quality of a product, the manager could seek for an alternative material composite (that is more sustainable, recyclable, and less hazardous) which could be lighter, and hence, this will reduce transportation cost (more economical) and the new product is more environment friendly due to the material used, and furthermore, eliminating health

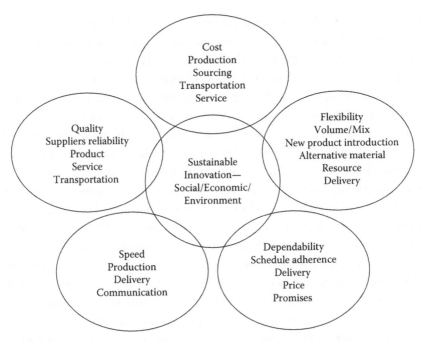

FIGURE 9.3
Innovation for performance measurements with sustainability agenda.

risks to the workers especially during the manufacturing stage. This could also be applied to the design of the packaging itself and the material used.

Adversely, if one has decided to increase the speed of delivering the demanded batch of products to the customers by extending working hours with the existing workforce, expanding the production economic runs, or increasing the fleet size or delivery frequency (and not achieving economic truckloads), then it is obvious that the overall cost will increase, workers' well-being will be compromised, and more waste could be produced due to the additional resources to meet the demands. In this scenario, sustainability agenda will play a key role for a more sustainable solution to be developed.

To further discuss the potential of innovation to meet sustainability agenda, we will again use technology innovation and innovative operations improvement as discussed in Chapter 4 in order to comprehend the synergy between innovation and sustainability.

As for technology innovation, we have discussed radio-frequency identification (RFID) technology, which is an excellent tool to replace repetitive, unproductive functions, for example, stock counts, and integrated with robotics systems to handle operations that are hazardous for humans. RFID can also be innovatively integrated with sensors and Internet of Things (IoT) to track sustainability indicators for instant alert of deviations. This piece of data can then be analyzed by big data analytics for continuous sustainability performance improvement. With a long list of IT systems as described in Chapter 4, an innovative sustainability-integrated operations improvement system can be developed. Hence, sustainability agenda can then be easily deployed and monitored to ensure the three dimensions are met.

Each operations improvement tool and technique discussed in Chapter 4 can be used innovatively and collectively to develop sustainable operations systems. For instance, value stream mapping could be developed focussing on sustainability values (and the non-values), and Lean approach will be a good way to reduce resources like nonrenewable energy and indecomposable materials for products. Business process reengineering (BPR) is ultimately promoting new thinking of redesigning business processes, and in this way, we can include the sustainability agenda at the beginning of process/product development stage. Not to mention that 5s, MUDA, and Poka-Yoke method are all good tools to reduce waste and meet other sustainability targets.

In terms of measuring sustainability performance/indicators, Section 9.3 examines different initiatives and tools for different operations, and other quality tools, such as cause and effect diagrams, statistical process control, Pareto analysis, flowcharts, control charts, are also good for measurement. However, in most occasions, these measurements take place in isolation. To effectively address truly and wholly the sustainability agenda, it is necessary to develop a framework that can assess the entire operations within the managers' role. As a matter of fact, it should track, monitor, and act on sustainability targets at strategic and operational levels. To begin on this journey, operations managers could start with some existing performance models, such as EFQM, Business Excellence Model, Malcolm Baldrige Quality Model, and eventually develop one that is suitable for their business environment.

9.6 SUMMARY

This chapter discussed a key term in the recent business environment, namely, *sustainability*, which has gained a significant attention in recent years by the industrialists as well as the research community. Fundamentally, there are three dimensions of sustainability, that is, social, environmental, and economic (SEE). These dimensions shall be concurrently considered and addressed in all aspects of operations management in any organization in order to be termed as a sustainable company. Obviously, this is a huge challenge and the knowledge of sustainability as well as the associated initiatives shall be mastered.

Various aspects of sustainability have been explored in this chapter, together with its synergy with innovation, which is the key focus of this book. This chapter discussed the development of sustainability and its crucial transformation targets, and followed by the existing initiatives attempting to achieve sustainability. Innovation is playing a key role in achieving true sustainability and the connection between the two was discussed with some examples provided. To provide consistency in building the knowledge, the approaches of innovative thinking and design in achieving sustainability were discussed using the same performance measurements and improvement tools used in Chapter 4.

The discussion in this entire chapter aims to help operations managers to see the more practical side of sustainability initiatives, together with innovative thinking, to achieve more sustainable economy, sustainable environment, and sustainable society.

KEY POINTS TO REMEMBER

- The term sustainability incorporates three key dimensions/pillars, namely, social, environmental, and economic.
- There might be some variants of definitions, but sustainability is still revolving around the three dimensions.
- Corporate social responsibility is not equal to sustainability, but only the social aspect of sustainability.
- Sustainability initiates involved transformation of traditional approach of resources/materials utilization resulting in high disposal of materials to minimal disposal and high reusability.
- There are identified challenges in achieving sustainability to be addressed.
- There is a long list of existing operations improvement tools and techniques as well as performance models, which can be used to achieve sustainability agenda and for sustainability performance measurements.
- Innovation plays a key part in achieving sustainability and the connection between the two shall be explored as an enabler for sustainability performance.

CASE STUDY

Power of Big Data in Forming a Quick
Sustainable Business Process

Simon Peter Nadeem

PhD Candidate, University of Derby, United Kingdom

Kristina Kim

Marketing Specialist, Kyrgyzstan

INTRODUCTION

As this chapter discusses innovation and sustainability, their driving forces, and synergy between them, this case study focuses on the vital role that data, and its analysis, play to draw an equal impact of innovation along with sustainability. Such is the case for ZEBRA Coffee & Snacks.

The business idea to establish Coffee Kiosk Networks in universities in Bishkek, Kyrgyzstan, was developed and implemented by the authors during their university education. The idea was initially sparked to establish a student-led business by franchising a well-known coffee brand in the country. Initial discussions with the franchisor enabled the move to proceed with the purchasing of equipment ordered from Italy as it would take few weeks before it could arrive. While the equipment was on its way and payments had been made, an issue was brought up by a direct competitor being a major buyer of coffee beans from the franchisor. This resulted in a smooth breakup initiated by the franchisor, with agreement that it would act as a supplier but not as a franchisor. This led to a complete chaos just eight weeks before the launch of the business. For this reason, the whole business plan needed to be worked out independently as well as to establish a brand while facing fierce competition. The choices were limited to either *give up* or *go ahead*. The business partners decided to go ahead.

In short time, a complete new detailed business plan, workout strategies, market analysis, branding, design of the shop's layout, and so on had to be developed. This was not an easy task given the

(Continued)

time and financial constraints, mingled with the lack of expertise, knowledge, and experience of the authors establishing and running a business of this type.

The business partners needed a survey analysis done at university level in at least five major universities. This required time, money, and manpower. To overcome these challenges, an ongoing MBA class of Management Consulting was approached, and with the agreement of the class tutor the project was designed and given to the students of this MBA course as a group assignment, dividing the class into three groups. This was a big move, as it resulted in a quick and large survey that included 500 students from five different universities. The three groups analyzed the data and developed the business plans, and each group presented it in a final presentation within eight days of the task being given.

The survey and the results obtained from its analysis helped the two partners to get an insight into the market and possible strategies, which then they mingled with their own thoughts to later establish the brand *ZEBRA Coffee & Snacks* with the slogan *Have fun with Zebra.*

The role of big data in formulating a business strategy that would result in a successful and sustainable business was remarkable as the business faced some common challenges related to the starting up of a new business. In this case, the big data helped the partners to address questions such as:

1. What is the market expectation in terms of product price, variety, and service level?
2. How can the business establish a brand name that would be meaningful and relevant to the student society?

(Continued)

3. How to keep the business profitable without going beyond the planned investment?
4. How to keep the business sustainable in all three economic, environmental, and social dimensions?

These challenges/problems were resolved in light of the data analysis in the following manner:

1. The survey results from the three groups and the proposed business plan by the MBA class helped to get an insight into the market potential and threats as well as possible strategies for success.
2. The brand name chosen by the authors was *ZEBRA*, being a catchy attraction as this animal has no direct affiliation with coffee. This attracted the question *Why Zebra*? Our answer was twofold:
   a. Zebra is a social animal and lives in groups, therefore we intend to promote and provide a socializing experience through the outlet;
   b. Each Zebra's stripe being unique means that we value each customer uniquely and each coffee sold was not the same to others.
3. Forming a strategic and exclusive agreement with the suppliers resulted in formulating a low cost strategy to be profitable while keeping the prices initially lower, and later similar to those of the competitors. Promotional discounts further added on to increased sales.
4. *Environmental*: Due to the outlet serving customers in a takeaway form, it was difficult to avoid the usage of paper cups and be environment friendly. However, the business promoted the usage of customers' own reusable cups by providing discounts. Also the participation in the promotion of university-wide Green Week was another effort to be environment friendly. The business ensured the recycling of bean bags and paper-based material to the maximum possible extent.

Social: Refer to point 2(b) above. Moreover the Kiosk contributed with small donations toward the student scholarship fund of the university.

(Continued)

Economic: Refer to point 3 above.

The quick efforts, mass data collection and analysis, and the formation of strategy resulted into a successful innovative and sustainable venture.

REFERENCES

Burnes, B. (2003). Managing change and changing managers from ABC to XYZ. *Journal of Management Development* 22(7): 627–642.

Carter, C.R. and Rogers, D.S. (2008). A framework of sustainable supply chain management: Moving toward new theory. *International Journal of Physical Distribution & Logistics Management* 38(5): 360–387.

Galbreath, J. (2009). Building corporate social responsibility into strategy. *European Business Review* 21(1): 109–127.

Garcia, S., Cintra, Y.C., Torres, R.D.S.R., Lima, F.G. (2016). Corporate sustainability management: A proposed multi-criteria model to support balanced decision-making. *Journal of Cleaner Production* 136: 181–196.

Klewitz, J. and Hansen, E.G. (2014). Sustainability-oriented innovation of SMEs: A systematic review. *Journal of Cleaner Production* 65: 57–75.

Law, K.M.Y. and Gunasekaran, A. (2012). Sustainability development in high-tech manufacturing firms in Hong Kong: Motivators and readiness. *International Journal of Production Economics* 137: 116–125.

Rushton, A., Croucher, P., Baker, P. (2014). *The Handbook of Logistics and Distribution Management*, 5th ed. London, UK: Kogan Page.

Simas, M.J.B.G.C., Lengler, J.F.B., António, N.J.S. (2013). Integration of sustainable development in the strategy implementation process: Proposal of a model. *Corporate Governance* 13(5): 511–526.

Vom Brocke, J., Seidel, S., Recker, J. (2012). *Green Business Process Management: Towards the Sustainable Enterprise*. Heidelberg, Germany: Springer.

WCED (1987). *Our Common Future: The Brundtland Report 1987*. Oxford, UK: World Commission on Environment and Development.

FURTHER SUGGESTED READINGS

Robertson, M. (2014). *Sustainability Principles and Practice*. Oxon, UK: Routledge.

Madhavan, G., Oakley, B., Green, D., Koon, D., Low, P. (Eds.) (2013). *Practicing Sustainability*. New York, NY: Springer-Verlag.

10

Going Beyond Managing—Improving Existing Services and Processes

10.1 INTRODUCTION

As the protective tissue separating the world's markets dissolves, as globalization has eroded the protective layer that separated the world markets, organizations have now been exposed to the power of competitors, which have not simply practiced the art of effectively designing, planning, and controlling their operations, but also to the power of those that continuously improve them. Thus, nowadays is key for operations managers, and their organizations, to go beyond simply being effective and efficient in managing their operations by also continuously seeking their improvement. The key is to develop a long-term improvement path rather than simply being good at managing operations. This philosophy and approach to operations are well embedded in *world-class* organizations such as General Electric and Toyota, and for many, this has been one of the main contributing factors to their success. Therefore, after having focused, in previous chapters, on different aspects mainly related to the management of innovative operations, this chapter focuses on their improvement. In particular, this chapter starts by discussing the need for going beyond the activity of simply managing operations, and then compares two opposite strategies in the *improvement spectrum* of operations, that is, continuous improvement and operational innovation. This chapter finishes by presenting and discussing some of the most commonly used triggers, that is, tools and techniques of innovation, which also enable the improvement of operations.

The key is to develop a long-term improvement path—rather than glean quick-hits from the latest fad.

10.2 GOING BEYOND THE MANAGEMENT OF OPERATIONS

In this book, in previous chapters so far we have argued the role that operations managers play in the (1) design, (2) management (i.e., planning and control), and (3) improvement of an organization's operations. We also agree with the fact that these activities are not only important for the effective and efficient functioning of an organization but also for its operations. However, increasing competitive pressure to sustain in the global market has resulted in a huge emphasis on the improvement of an organization's operations that fall within the responsibilities of operations managers. It is well evident that to compete globally, sustaining performance is not enough and organizations need to strive hard for continuous improvement. Failure to continuously improve will result in the loss of profit and market share, as competitors will catch up if they are on the path of continuous improvement. We have discussed in detail earlier in Chapter 5 the role of all operations managers in creating a culture of innovation and continuous improvement to support their organization in its constant battle for competitiveness. Operations managers therefore continuously need to devise new and innovative ways for improving operations. However, the key question that demands attention is: How can they trigger an investigation that results in an improvement? In this direction, Trott (2017) put forward the idea of identifying and utilizing techniques that can help start this improvement process. In the upcoming sections of this chapter, we review the two most commonly used strategies to improvement and some techniques that trigger innovation.

10.3 STRATEGIES TO IMPROVEMENT

Devising a strategy/approach for continuous improvement is vital for operations managers. The selection of the right strategy/approach is mostly aligned with the culture of the organization whether the culture is geared toward operational innovation or continuous improvement (see Chapter 5). These two improvement strategies, breakthrough improvements (i.e., operational innovation) and continuous improvement, are based on different philosophies and to a certain extent are opposite. The primary difference between operational innovation and continuous improvement strategies, within an operations context, is that although the main focus of the first is to conduct improvements based on breakthrough/radical operational innovations, the second adopts an approach to improving operations that follows constant, smaller, and endless incremental steps. Table 10.1 summarizes some of the main differences between these two improvement strategies.

TABLE 10.1

Differences between Operational Innovation and Continuous Based Improvement Strategies

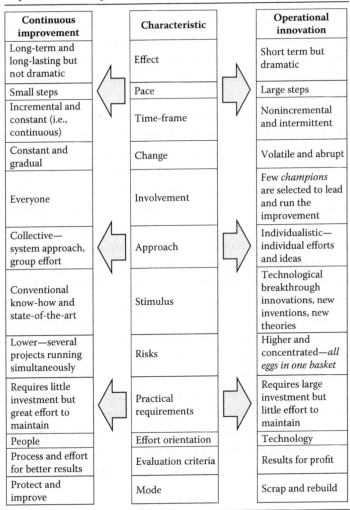

Continuous improvement	Characteristic	Operational innovation
Long-term and long-lasting but not dramatic	Effect	Short term but dramatic
Small steps	Pace	Large steps
Incremental and constant (i.e., continuous)	Time-frame	Nonincremental and intermittent
Constant and gradual	Change	Volatile and abrupt
Everyone	Involvement	Few *champions* are selected to lead and run the improvement
Collective—system approach, group effort	Approach	Individualistic—individual efforts and ideas
Conventional know-how and state-of-the-art	Stimulus	Technological breakthrough innovations, new inventions, new theories
Lower—several projects running simultaneously	Risks	Higher and concentrated—*all eggs in one basket*
Requires little investment but great effort to maintain	Practical requirements	Requires large investment but little effort to maintain
People	Effort orientation	Technology
Process and effort for better results	Evaluation criteria	Results for profit
Protect and improve	Mode	Scrap and rebuild

Source: Adapted from Slack, N. et al., *Operations Management*, 8th ed., Pearson, Harlow, UK, 2016.

10.3.1 An Operational Innovation or a Continuous Improvement Strategy?

The choice between operational innovation and continuous improvement strategy at this stage could be difficult to realize for operations managers. The reason behind this dilemma could be attributed to the fact that if both strategies are well planned, executed, and aligned with operational strategy, then they should yield the same expected benefits to the organization. However, evidence suggests that in many cases, the expectations for improvements through operational innovations are higher than the results achieved and this is a very common phenomenon in the industry. The higher expectations may occur because there is normally a large capital investment associated with these types of improvements, for example, investment in a new multimillion production machine can lead to a large improvement in the production volume and capacity utilization in a production line.

Although one would expect that organizations would normally choose one of the improvement strategies discussed earlier, however it is possible to merge and create a "hybrid" strategy. For example, within the automotive industry, Toyota is well known for fiercely pursuing continuous improvements in their operations following the Deming's plan–do–check–act (i.e., PDCA) improvement cycle, which is a part of its already well-embedded kaizen (i.e., continuous improvement) culture and approach to improvement. However, Toyota recognizes that in certain circumstances, it is necessary to complement and combine the incremental improvements with operational innovations that radically improve or even completely redesign certain aspects of its processes in a short period of time. The combination of radical (i.e., operational innovation) and incremental (i.e., continuous improvement) improvement initiatives is a common practice in many organizations as reported in the work of Grover and Kettinger (1998). For example, organizations may innovate by radically designing new operations, but then may implement short-term incremental improvements on this operation. This suggests that both improvement strategies are perfectly compatible and their combination often yields better result. Therefore, operations managers should aim at developing the cultural characteristics and elements (see Chapter 5) supporting the effective adoption of both strategies.

10.3.2 Improvement Cycle Models

Improvement is an endless process as perfection is never achieved and hence there is always room for further improvement. This is the cornerstone thinking to the continuous improvement philosophy. The endless nature of continuous improvement is usually represented through the idea of an improvement cycle and there are many improvement or problem-solving methodologies based on such cycles. The work of Garza-Reyes et al. (2014) provides a good review of some of the most commonly used improvement cycles in the industry, but many of them are proprietary models developed and owned by consultancy companies. Two most common and well-known improvement cycles are, PDCA cycle developed by the quality guru W.E. Deming and the define, measure, analyze, improve, and control (DMAIC) cycle, made popular by the well-recognized Six Sigma approach. The rigorous, systematic, and disciplined structure and approach to improvement makes these two improvement cycles very effective, a fact that has been well acknowledged by most business excellence and process improvement specialists. These improvement cycles provide a step-by-step approach to solve the problem to achieve improvement while simultaneously establishing a standardized routine to improvement and problem solving. Figure 10.1 illustrates the PDCA and DMAIC improvement cycles, and a set of activities that needs to be carried out in every stage of the cycle.

There is no specific guidance for operations managers with regard to the selection of PDCA or the DMAIC improvement cycle for the improvement efforts. However, it has been evidenced that where Six Sigma or Lean Six Sigma has been adopted, operations managers tend to prefer DMAIC over PDCA. For example, the Civil Aerospace division of the UK's and East Midlands-based major manufacturer of aero engines Rolls-Royce uses DMAIC as it has adopted the Six Sigma approach, whereas operations managers working for companies where Six Sigma has not been embedded tend to use the PDCA cycle, such as the case of Toyota, UK. Regardless of the preferences in certain situations, the literature in relation to the use and application of both improvement cycles tends to suggest that none of them is better than the other. This indicates that both are very suitable to guide the improvement efforts of operations managers. In order to improve your understanding and more detailed information

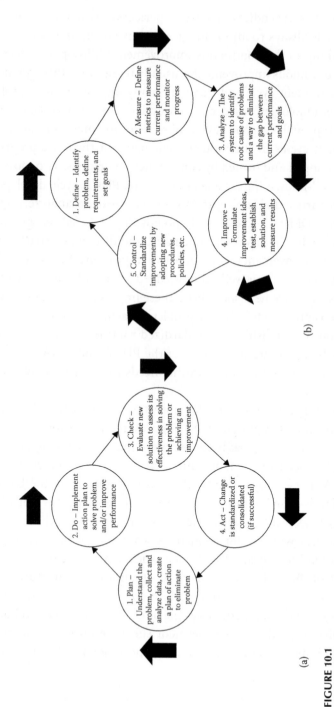

FIGURE 10.1

The (a) Deming's PDCA improvement cycle and the (b) Six Sigma's DMAIC improvement cycle.

regarding how any of these two improvement cycles could provide you with a roadmap for improvement, you can refer to the works of Shankar (2009), George (2002), Carroll (2013), and Pyzdek and Keller (2009) for DMAIC; and Imai (2012), Basu (2004), Alukal and Manos (2006), and Chiarini (2012) for PDCA.

10.4 TRIGGERS OF INNOVATION

In the previous section, we have discussed how operations managers can guide the improvement of their processes by following an improvement cycle such as PDCA or DMAIC. However, before that occurs, a starting point for analysis should be determined. An excellent starting point would be the customer itself. It has to be remembered that the ultimate objective of every organization should always be to meet, or even exceed, the needs and requirements of its customers. At the end of the day, the mere reason for an organization to exist is its customers, so they determine the bare survival and success/failure of the company. It is therefore of paramount importance for operations managers to consider the customers of their organizations as the starting point for any improvement initiatives and activities. In this line, quality performance is one of the key responsibilities of operations management, so improving performance in this area is critical to all companies. We briefly review some of the most common techniques used in industry by operations managers to improve the quality of their products and services in the following sections.

10.4.1 Gap Analysis

It is very important for operations managers to fully understand their customers and their expectations to produce and deliver quality products/services meeting those expectations. Since customer preferences and expectations vary and also changes over time, this makes evaluation of customer's expectations very difficult. For example, 20 years ago, cars were not as efficient, environmental friendly, and reliable as today's latest models. Today's buyers (i.e., users) expect a car with a very low cost of fuel consumption per mile (i.e., efficient), a car that does not break (i.e., reliable), and a car that produces a very low CO_2 emission (i.e., environmental friendly). This is a very different expectation compared to 20 years ago.

Gap analysis is one of the most extensively used techniques to find out whether there is a gap between the customer's expectation of a product or service and their perception. Nowadays this technique is used to determine whether there is a performance problem in a product or service and once a problem has been identified, an operations manager can either follow radical improvement approach based on an operational innovation to solve it or an improvement cycle approach like PDCA or DMAIC to tackle it in an incremental manner.

Consider the example given in Figure 10.2 of an engineering student (i.e., customer) who is expecting to operate an *easy to learn and use* simulation software. The expectations of the engineering student are based upon the simulation software developer's and software's version, experience, and word of mouth exchanges. These in combination may result in the engineering student having a *specification* of what he or she means by an easy to learn and use simulation software. On the other hand, the software developer through the software designers has a concept of what easy to learn and use means for a specific software's version. Some differences and gaps are shown in Figure 10.2. This is important as every gap is a source of a student's (i.e., customer's) dissatisfaction with the simulation software's developer. Thus, every one of these gaps represents an opportunity

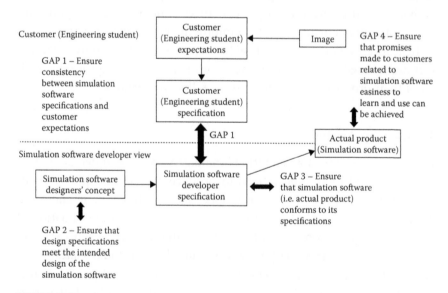

FIGURE 10.2

Quality gap analysis. (Adapted from Trott, P., *Innovation Management and New Product Development*, 6th ed., Pearson, Harlow, UK, 2017.)

for improvement, in this case, either to the simulation software's design team, which needs to align the product's requirement to what the customer is expecting, or to the marketing team, which needs to manage the expectation of the customers more effectively. For this, an improvement, or corrective action plan, needs to be formulated and implemented by the simulation software developer to make sure that the negative gap between customers' expectations and perceptions is eliminated. Indeed, in this era of fierce competition it is not enough to simply close the gap between these two, but organizations must actually strive to exceed the expectations of their customers. This will not only ensure the survival of an organization but it will also greatly contribute to the achievement of its leadership in its market.

More detailed information on how to conduct a performance gap analysis can be found in the work of Franklin (2006).

10.4.2 Benchmarking

Once the gap between the customer's expectations and perceptions has been identified by operations managers, the next step should be to close/eliminate this gap through operational performance improvement. Benchmarking is one of the techniques widely used by operations managers and organizations to accomplish this. It is normally understood as an approach employed by operations managers to set performance standards by comparing the operations of their own organizations with those of another organization, or even with other parts within their own organization. Usually, the comparison is done with world leaders or best in class organizations, which helps operations managers understand the best practices and operation methods that can help them to achieve the same best-in-class performance. Slack et al. (2016) referred this benchmarking approach as *the process of learning from others*.

Benchmarking approach developed by Rank Xerox in 1975 comprises of ten activities and five stages that operations managers must carry out. These activities and stages are illustrated in Figure 10.3, which corresponds to a comparison between two, or more, organizations (i.e., external benchmarking). This process can be easily adapted by operations managers at microlevel to compare the internal operational performance, for example, of two different production lines within the same company. This is referred as *internal benchmarking*, which is widely practiced by many organizations. For example, Toyota follows internal benchmarking process to learn

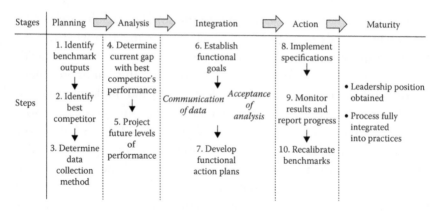

FIGURE 10.3
Benchmarking process as developed by Xerox.

from the best practices followed in its other manufacturing plants around Europe by comparing them with their UK car assembly plant.

Readers interested to explore more detailed information about benchmarking can refer to the work of Stapenhurst (2009), Andersen and Pettersen (1996), and Codling (1996).

10.4.3 Quality Circles

Another technique normally employed by organizations to eliminate the gap between customer's expectation and perception of a product or service is *quality circle*. A quality circle is a small group of workers, which meet voluntarily and regularly to discuss and collectively propose solutions to operational problems faced by their departments and organizations. This idea of collective work to improvement is inspired from the philosophies of quality gurus such as Deming, Ishikawa, and Juran, who believed that getting quality right and also improving it are the responsibilities of all employees. This idea also departs from the general belief that shop-floor employees who spend most of their day carrying out certain operational activities can therefore be considered the experts of what they do. These experts are more likely to find a faster and more effective solution to their work problems if they work collectively. Therefore, quality circle aims to tackle and solve the operational and quality problems identified through the gap analysis by encouraging team work.

Literature is abundant with success stories of the quality circles technique. Literature indicates that over 10 million Japanese workers by being part of the improvement teams have contributed to save several thousand

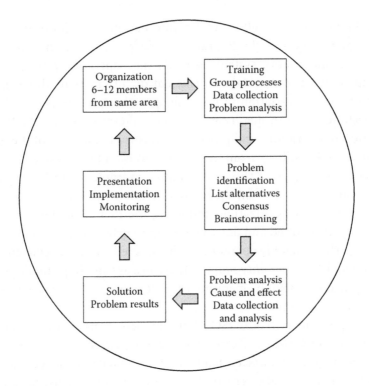

FIGURE 10.4
Process to form and run quality circles improvement projects.

U.S. dollars to their organizations by improving their operations, products, and/or their services (Russel and Taylor, 2003). Large organizations such as Tata Steel and Du Pont have also reported very significant improvements in their operations after the implementation of quality circles. Figure 10.4 illustrates the formation and operation process that operations managers can follow to form quality circles teams and operate effectively.

Readers expecting further insights on quality circles can refer to the work of Basu (2004) and Robson (1988).

10.4.4 The ISO 9000 Approach

ISO 9000 is another one of the common approaches to maintain competitiveness through the provision of quality products and services used by organizations. International Standards Organization, ISO 9000 was introduced in the late 1980s (1987) and has since evolved over several revisions. ISO 9000 is a set of international standards on quality management and quality assurances to help organizations effectively document the quality system elements (i.e., operations/processes) to be implemented to maintain an efficient quality system. This helps in the reduction of variation in how the operation/process is performed. It is well accepted in quality management literature that reduction of variation in operations and processes improves the quality of the product or service resulting from those operations and processes. There are numerous examples of this and a simple example could be drawn at an operational level of an assembly operation performed by a shop-floor employee. Organizations following the ISO 9000 standards will have a clearly defined and documented approach in a *quality manual* to carry out this assembly operation in the most effective and efficient way. Documentation in *quality manual* therefore assists shop-floor employees engaged in assembly operation to perform such activities with same highly defined standards.

The implementation of an ISO 9000 approach seems to be more aligned with the characteristics of a mechanistic organization, which seeks efficiency in its operations (see Chapter 6). ISO 9000 has also received criticism that it may hinder creativity and innovation because it requires employees to follow standard and rigid procedures, instead of finding novel and innovative ways to perform operations and processes, which may result in the definition of new best practices. However despite these criticisms, ISO approach has remained popular and has been adopted by millions of organizations from various industrial sectors across the globe. Besides defining and documenting operations and processes, ISO 9000 intends to anticipate the possible quality problems that the organization may face, thus it is also considered as a quality assurance framework. How ISO 9000 tackles common quality issues is shown in Table 10.2.

As evident from the previous discussions, ISO 9000 approach assures improved quality of products and services. However, ISO 9000 also appears to support the continuous improvement culture, for example, through the PDCA improvement cycle. The standard documentation procedures of best practices required by ISO 9000 can serve as *door stop* to ensure that an organization sustains the improvement (i.e., best practices) following the PDCA improvement cycle. Failure to document the new best

TABLE 10.2

ISO 9000 Approach to Addressing Quality Issues

Common Quality Problem	How ISO 9000 Addresses a Problem?
Quality is not considered by employees as their responsibility	You emphasize the importance of quality for the organization and place responsibility for it on those who provide the service or produce the product
Communication between departments is poor, or not existent at all	You ensure that employees of different functional areas of the organization communicate effectively and that communication barriers are eliminated
Unacceptable service or faulty goods are provided to customers, resulting in their expectations not being met and their dissatisfaction	You establish and carry out proper inspection checks, investigate the root cause of the problem, and formulate a strategy for its elimination and continuous improvement
The correct person is not involved in the decision-making process and thus errors are made	You specify the precise person who is responsible for the operation/process and its quality
Mistakes arise because of the lack of proper training to employees	You provide training to your employees so they know what their job is and how to perform it
Mistakes are uncorrected when found, hence the same mistakes are made and keep reappearing regularly	You analyze the mistakes so the root cause is understood and these are corrected. Then you set in place mechanisms to prevent the same errors from reoccurring again
Variations in product and services' quality are caused by different employees making the same product or providing the same service following their own way of doing things	You identify and define best practices in doing an operation or process, adopt such best practices, and make sure that they are consistently followed by all employees
Wrong products or information are produced and given because people are using specifications which are out-of-date	You make sure that everyone uses the most up-to-date version of a document by putting in place a control process for documents

practices may leave the organization back to the old practices and they may be left behind their competitors. A diagrammatic representation of this is shown in Figure 10.5.

More detailed discussion on ISO 9000 can be found in the work of Hoyle (2009), Seaver (2001), and Self and Roche (2007).

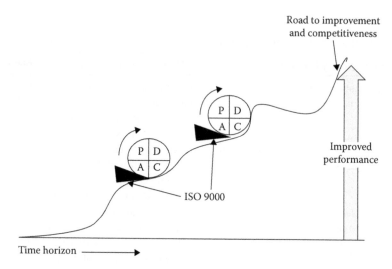

FIGURE 10.5
Role of ISO 9000 in continuous improvement.

10.4.5 Total Quality Management

Total quality management (TQM) is one of the most well-known quality management approaches and its application is not only confined to the operations function of an organization but its philosophy and principles are equally applicable to marketing, human resources, and any other organizational functions. Compared to the previously discussed approaches, TQM is an organization-wide approach that requires implementation from a strategic viewpoint rather than from an operational one. Therefore, in an organization that has embarked on a TQM journey, operations managers need to ensure that all the ideas and philosophies followed by TQM are embedded within the heart and minds of their employees.

Management literature is abundant with the success and failure stories of organizations following the TQM approach, where success stories show how TQM has helped organizations to improve the quality of their products and services as well as their competitiveness. On the other hand, many studies report *bitter* experiences of organizations where TQM implementation has led to disappointing results. However, most, if not all, failures have been linked to the implementation aspect of TQM, and not to its philosophy and principles. There are good evidences documented in literature to show that if effectively adopted by organizations, TQM principles should make organizations more competitive by meeting and in some cases exceeding customer's needs and expectations. A summary of key principles supported by TQM and other technique and tools is presented in Table 10.3.

Readers interested to gain further insights into TQM can refer to the work of Bagad (2008), Besterfield et al. (2011), and Oakland (2003).

TABLE 10.3

Philosophies Stressed by TQM

Philosophy/Principle	Tools/Techniques
1. Meeting the needs and expectations of customers • Quality is determined by the customer • *Customer is god*	• Gap analysis • Voice of the customer • Customer surveys • Listening to customers' complaints • Kano model • Focus groups • Interviews
2. Covering the entire (all parts of the) organization	• Engaging every employee within the organization • Concept of internal customer—internal supplier • Management by walking about
3. Every person in the organization contributes to quality	• Gaining full commitment from employees to understand that every job position and functional area within an organization contribute to quality • Engaging every employee within the organization • Quality circles

4. All costs of quality are considered
• *Quality is free*
	• Cost of quality is considered and classified as:
	  • *Prevention cost*—activities that ensure right first time performance
	  • *Appraisal cost*—activities that check whether right first time is achieved
	  • *Internal failure*—internal activities, which result from not conforming to right first time
	  • *External failure*—after change of ownership or at the customer, activities that result from not conforming to right first time

5. Getting things right at the first time	• Zero defects • Poka-yokes
6. Developing the systems and procedures, which support quality and improvement	• Quality standards (e.g., ISO 9000, etc.) • Company quality manual • Procedures manual • Work instructions, specifications, and detail methods for performing activities
7. Developing a continuous improvement culture	• Improvement cycles (e.g., PDCA, DMAIC, etc.)

10.4.6 Business Excellence Models—The EFQM Business Excellence Model

Business excellence models (BEMs) are one of the popular quality management frameworks that have evolved from the TQM principles. BEMs are developed based on organizational performance criteria across different areas of a business that are considered to be a benchmark for excellence. The success and effectiveness of BEMs in improving the competitiveness of organizations are well documented with the quality foundations that administer those BEMs across regions and countries (e.g., European Foundation for Quality Management—Europe, the National Institute of Science and Technology—U.S., The Japanese Institute of Scientist and Engineers—Japan, among others). It is estimated that more than 83 countries have their own version of BEMs and some of the examples of BEMs include the European Foundation for Quality Management (EFQM) model (Europe), Malcolm Baldrige National Quality Award (U.S.), and Deming Prize (Japan).

In order to understand the BEMs and their contribution to improvement of organizations operations and business performance, let us focus on the EFQM model. The structure of the EFQM model is shown in Figure 10.6, which shows the underlying performance areas (employee satisfaction, customer satisfaction, impact on society, and business results) that organizations must aim to achieve excellence. Although these four result factors are important, they have different contributions to excellence. As a result

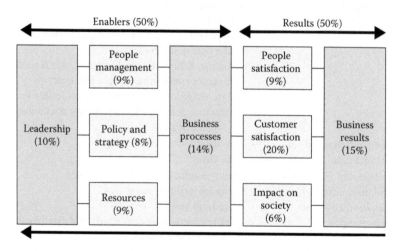

FIGURE 10.6
Criteria structure of the EFQM model.

they are given different weights in EFQM models. In EFQM model the result is achieved through five enablers (leadership, people management, policy and strategy, resources, and business processes). These enablers also have a different level of contribution to achieve those results. Therefore, organizations following EFQM model must stimulate these five enablers to achieve results across the four performance measures.

BEMs have been used for different purposes including award participation, measurement systems, and strategic planning; however, operations managers can use their criteria for self-assessment and process improvement. A self-assessment approach based on the use of a BEM can provide an organization with a powerful approach to understand how it is performing against excellence criterion and to identify the areas in need of improvement. This is the prime benefit of the use of a BEM at operational level and when used as a self-assessment tool. It is worth noting that competing for award is not necessary for organizations, but is necessary to simply take the criteria for excellence established by the model, to use it for measuring their performance, and to identify the gaps between the model criteria and the performance of the organization. This will help organizations to highlight areas that need improvement leading to the formulation of an improvement agenda and strategy, for example, using the improvement strategies, improvement cycles, and/or techniques previously reviewed, to close the gap between the model criteria and the performance of the organization. A roadmap based on best practices, to carry out a self-assessment exercise using a BEM, has been suggested by Rocha-Lona et al. (2013). You can follow their advice and recommendations if you wish to try it in your organization.

Readers interested to explore further about BEMs can refer to the works of Porter and Tanner (2012), Bansal et al. (2015), Kanji (2005), and Hakes (2007), or can visit the website of the European Foundation for Quality Management (http://www.efqm.org/) for further details on EFQM model.

10.5 SUMMARY

This chapter focused on an activity that nowadays has taken a prominent position in the role of operations managers, that is, the improvement of operations. Since it is not enough in the modern competitive environment to simply be effective and efficient in designing, planning, and controlling operations, operations managers must strive and seek ways to constantly improve them. An organizational culture where continuous improvement is a cornerstone of the day-to-day operations of a company and operational innovation is a part of its strategy will ensure its survival and competitiveness. In this chapter we have therefore emphasized this fact as our industrial experience indicates that even in the modern and competitive globalized environment of the twenty-first century, continuous improvement and operational innovation are not always constantly pursued, and/or even considered, in many organizations, especially small- and medium-sized enterprises. We have also discussed two *extreme* and opposite strategies to improvement such as continuous improvement and operational innovation and exposed their different characteristics. However, despite being different approaches to improve operations, we have also emphasized the fact that rather than a company selecting one or the other, organizations should combine them according to their different requirements and specific situations as both are complementary to the other. We have also discussed the PDCA and DMAIC continuous improvement cycle models, which nowadays are the two most commonly used approaches that organizations use to guide their efforts through an endless cycle of continuous improvement. Finally, some specific triggers of innovation and enablers of operational improvement such as gap analysis, benchmarking, quality circles, and ISO standards, among others, are also discussed. Although every single improvement strategy, improvement cycle model, and tools and techniques presented in this chapter can be a broad topic on its own right, we hope the chapter presents a general overview, to people interested in operations improvement, of the importance and need for improving operations as well as the different ways for achieving this.

KEY POINTS TO REMEMBER

The role of operations managers centres in the (1) design, (2) management (i.e., planning and control), and (3) improvement of an organization's operations. All these activities are important for the functioning of an organization's operations. However, nowadays the activity of improving operations takes a prominent role within any organization.

- Two strategies that represent different, and until certain extent opposite, philosophies to improvement are breakthrough improvements (i.e., operational innovation) and continuous improvement.
- Both strategies to improvement are perfectly compatible and indeed to obtain better results they should be combined.
- Since perfection is never achieved and hence there is always room for improvement, this activity should be considered as an endless process. The endless nature of continuous improvement is usually represented through the idea of an improvement cycle. Examples of continuous improvement cycles include PDCA and DMAIC.
- Some of the most common techniques used in industry by operations managers to improve operations and the quality of their products and services include: gap analysis, benchmarking, quality circles, and ISO standards, among many others.

CASE STUDY

Finishing Process Improvement—Tension Leveller Productivity Improvement

Mustafa Al-Balushi

Six Sigma Master Black Belt at Oman Aluminum Rolling Company, Oman

INTRODUCTION

An aluminum-rolling mill plant consists of four main processing areas. It starts with remelt, casting and hot rolling mill, cold rolling mill, and finishing. In finishing, the coils are processed through tension-leveling machine before packing them as illustrated in Figure CS10.1. The productivity of each of the operation areas is crucial to ensure a leveled production flow in the plant. An improvement opportunity was identified in the tension leveler line performance. This was addressed through the four stages of the plan–do–check–act (PDCA) improvement cycle.

(Continued)

FIGURE CS10.1
Aluminum-rolling process.

PLAN STAGE

Business Case

Tension leveler line productivity is a key to maximize the production of finishing products, which has more value added to the business financials. Moreover, improving the productivity of this operation would eliminate the bottleneck phenomena found in the process.

Opportunity Statement

The average tension leveler line productivity was around 10 Master Coils/day and 70 Coils/week during the period from April 2016 to July 2016. This productivity level limited the monthly production of finished good tonnages to around 2000 MT only, which affected various aspects of the business (Figure CS10.2).

Objective

To increase the average productivity of the tension leveler line by 30%.

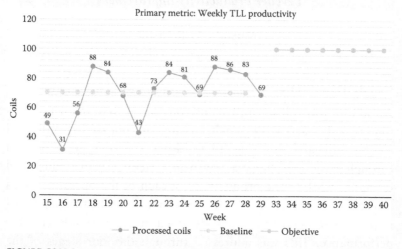

FIGURE CS10.2
Weekly tension-leveling line productivity.

(*Continued*)

Current Condition

Process mapping was used to define the process of processing the coil in the tension leveling line. The existing process is illustrated in Figure CS10.3. It starts with requesting the coil by the autocrane from the Coil Park. Then, the coil is loaded on the tension-leveling line machine. Some steps are completed before start processing the coil through the tension-leveling line, which are preparation, setup trims specifications, joining, threading, exit shear, tension setup, inspection, and removing scrap. All these steps are followed for every single coil process in the tension-leveling line.

Also, the process is summarized into three main categories, or stages, which are preparation stage, production stage, and coil changeover stage as shown in Figure CS10.4. Production stage is the only value-added activity in the process, whereas preparation and changeover stages are non-value-added activities. Measurement of the process was taken to help understand the distribution of existing wastes in the process. The current process showed an average performance of 2.2 hours/coil. Around 70% of the process was spent in the preparation stage as illustrated in the Pareto Chart in Figure CS10.5.

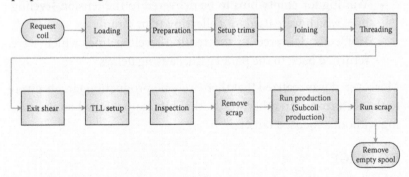

FIGURE CS10.3
Tension-leveling line process.

FIGURE CS10.4
Process macrolevel.

(Continued)

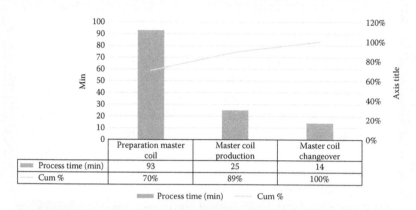

FIGURE CS10.5
Pareto chart.

Analyzing further the preparation stage, several reasons that led to delay time to complete the preparation stage for every coil were identified. The most frequent reasons that caused delays were the following:

- Waiting for the autocrane to bring the requested coil from the coil park
- Waiting for empty bins to be delivered to the tension-leveling line, which were used for collecting trim scrap
- Hot coils delivered to the tension-leveling line, which were returned back to the park again, causing delays

Moreover, it was realized that there were no production targets given to the shift teams. In other words, the shift team worked on producing without a focused target.

DO STAGE

Improvement ideas were generated through a brainstorming session. The improvement actions were as follows:

- Since there were three saddles, or spaces, for coils in front of the entry side in the tension-leveling line, all these saddles were to be filled with coils. This would reduce and eliminate the delay of waiting for the auto-crane to transfer the requested coil from the coil park.

(Continued)

- Keep consistently a minimum of two empty bins available as buffer during the operations. This would help in eliminating line stoppages.
- Check the coil temperature from production lot ticket or physically by using a thermogun device.
- Implement Lean daily meetings that would help to setup a management by objective approach and build performance management.

CHECK STAGE

After implementing the proposed improvement actions, the tension-leveling line productivity responded positively and increased production capacity from 70 Coils/week to around 100 Coils/week. This represented an improvement of around 30% in productivity as illustrated in Figures CS10.6 and CS10.7.

ACT

Control is a key to sustain the improvement made in any process. Therefore, the improvement actions were included in the operations

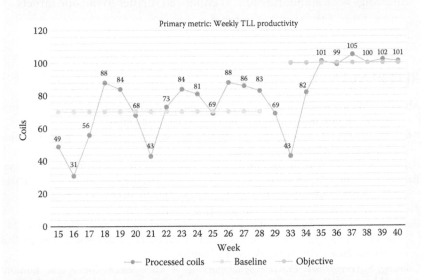

FIGURE CS10.6
Weekly tension-leveling line productivity.

(Continued)

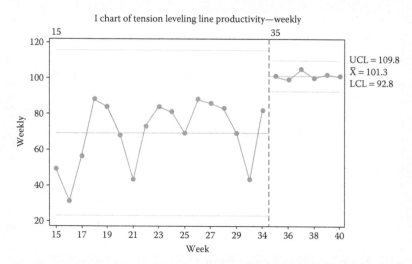

FIGURE CS10.7
Control chart of tension-leveling line productivity.

standard operating procedures (SOP). Moreover, a training was delivered to the shift teams on the new changes. In addition, Lean meetings were standardized and enhanced further to include targets and actions if the target is not met.

REFERENCES

Alukal, G., Manos, A. (2006). *Lean Kaizen: A Simplified Approach to Process Improvements American Society for Quality*. Milwaukee, WI: Quality Press.

Andersen, P., Pettersen, G. (1996). *Benchmarking Handbook, Step-by-step Instructions*. London, UK: Chapman and Hall.

Bagad, V.S. (2008). *Total Quality Management*. Pune, India: Technical Publications Pune.

Bansal, A., Phatak, Y., Sharma, R.K. (2015). *Quality Management Practices for Global Excellence*. Indore, India: Prestige Institute of Management and Research.

Basu, R. (2004). *Implementing Quality*. London, UK: Thompson.

Besterfield, D.H., Besterfield-Michna, C., Besterfield, G.H., Besterfield-Sacre, M., Urdhwareshe, H., Urdhwareshe, R. (2011). *Total Quality Management*, Revised 3rd Edition. New Delhi, India: Pearson Education.

Codling, S. (1996). *Best Practice Benchmarking: A Management Guide*, 2nd Edition. Aldershot, UK: Gower Press.

Carroll, C.T. (2013). *Six Sigma for Powerful Improvement: A Green Belt DMAIC Training System with Software Tools and a 25-Lesson Course*. Boca Raton, FL: Productivity Press.

Chiarini, A. (2012). *From Total Quality Control to Lean Six Sigma: Evolution of the Most Important Management Systems for the Excellence*. Heidelberg, Germany: Springer.

Franklin, M. (2006). *Performance Gap Analysis: Tips, Tools, and Intelligence for Trainers*. Scottsdale, AZ: ASTD Press.

Garza-Reyes J.A., Flint, A., Kumar, V., Antony, J., Soriano-Meier, H. (2014). A DMAIRC approach to lead time reduction in an aerospace engine assembly process. *Journal of Manufacturing Technology Management* 25(1): 27–48.

George, M. (2002). *Lean Six Sigma, Chapter 10—Implementation: The DMAIC Improvement Process*. Berkshire, UK: McGraw-Hill.

Grover, V., Kettinger, W.J. (1998). *Business Process Change: Reengineering Concepts, Methods and Technologies*. London, UK: Idea Group Publishing.

Hakes, C. (2007). *The EFQM excellence model for Assessing Organizational Performance*. Zaltbommel, the Netherlands: Best Practice Series Edition, Van Haren Publishing.

Hoyle, D. (2009). ISO 9000 *Quality Systems Handbook: Using the Standards as a Framework for Business Improvement*, 6th Edition. Oxford, UK: Butterworth-Heinemann.

Imai, M. (2012). *Gemba Kaizen: A Commonsense Approach to a Continuous Improvement Strategy*, 2nd Edition. Berkshire, UK: MacGraw-Hill.

Kanji, G.K. (2005). *Measuring Business Excellence*. New York, NY: Routledge.

Oakland, J.S. (2003). *Total Quality Management: Text with Cases*. Oxford, UK: Butterworth-Heinemann.

Porter, L., Tanner, S. (2012). *Assessing Business Excellence*, 2nd Edition. Oxford, UK: Butterworth-Heinemann.

Robson, M. (1988). *Quality Circles; A Practical Guide*, 2nd Edition. Aldershot, UK: Gower Press.

Rocha-Lona, L., Garza-Reyes, J.A., Kumar, V. (2013). *Building Quality Management Systems: Selecting the Right Methods and Tools*. Boca Raton, FL: Productivity Press.

Pyzdek, T., Keller, P. (2009). *The Six Sigma Handbook: A Complete Guide for Green Belts, Black Belts, and Managers at All Levels*, 3rd Edition. Berkshire, UK: McGraw-Hill.

Russel, R., Taylor, B. (2003). *Operations Management*. Hoboken, NJ: Prentice Hall, Englewood Cliffs.

Seaver, M. (2001). *Implementing ISO 9000:2000*. Aldershot, UK: Gower Press.

Self, B., Roche, G. (2007). *Customer Satisfaction Measurement for ISO 9000: 2000*. Oxford, UK: Butterworth-Heinemann.

Shankar, R. (2009). *Process Improvement Using Six Sigma: A DMAIC Guide*. Milwaukee, WI: American Society for Quality, Quality Press.

Slack, N., Brandon-Jones, A., Johnston, R. (2016). *Operations Management*, 8th Edition. Harlow, UK: Pearson.

Stapenhurst, T. (2009). *The Benchmarking Book: A How-to-guide to Best Practice for Managers and Practitioners*. Oxford, UK: Butterworth-Heinemann.

Trott, P. (2017). *Innovation Management and New Product Development*, 6th Edition. Harlow, UK: Pearson.

Index

Note: Page numbers followed by f and t refer to figures and tables, respectively.